Becoming a Leader

*How to Develop
Leadership*

by
Elmer L. Towns

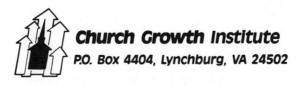

Church Growth Institute
P.O. Box 4404, Lynchburg, VA 24502

Table of Contents

FOREWORD

Dear Friends,

Leadership is the difference that builds a growing church. My good friend, Dr. Lee Robertson, has said, "Everything rises and falls on leadership." He told me that statement many years ago when I was in his office. Over the years, I have seen that great leaders have made a difference in growing a church. Some great leaders have been Pastors, Sunday School Superintendents, Bus Directors, and Sunday School Teachers. Today, lack of leadership is the missing gap that keeps many churches from reaching their potential.

As the Chancellor of a University, I want to train young leaders for the church of Jesus Christ. However, I realize that leadership is more than acquiring knowledge or gaining academic tools. That is why we apply the motto "action oriented curriculum." Leaders are formed in the crucible of service, not simply by sitting in a classroom.

I've seen students go through with a straight "A" average, yet never become the great leader that God meant them to be. At other times, I have seen "C" students excel as leaders. God has used them greatly in foreign missions, in education, or the pastorate.

What is the difference? Leadership is the total person who leads. Leadership involves spirituality, knowledge, skills, and accumulated experiences. Leadership gets results.

Mary Frances Johnson Preston first wrote four chapters of this book to train Sunday School teachers in leadership skills. This book was introduced to the Liberty Schools first by Gordon Luff who trained many youth directors and pastors in leadership skills. Dr. Towns has added to it some of the insights of leadership and uses it to train pastors. I recommend *Becoming a Leader* to fill the gap of leadership in your church.

Dr. Towns talks about the "Hot Poker" principle of Church Leaderhip. By that he means that young leaders learn leadership from great leaders. As the poker becomes hot when placed into the coals, so people become leaders by their exposure to the influence of great leaders.

Study this book to become a leader. Teach this book to your people to make them leaders. Apply this book to make your church grow; and in the process God will be glorified.

Sincerely,

Jerry Falwell

Jerry Falwell

CHAPTER ONE

DISCIPLES ARE LEADERS

Amerrica seems to be the home of popular Christianity. Approximately 42 per cent of the population claims to be a Christian. When taken on the surface, one would think that if 40 per cent of Americans profess faith in Christ, they would make a significant impact on the nation. One would think there would be a righteous influence on this nation so that there would not be a wide-spread use of alcohol or at least its widespread influence. One would think that there would not be nudity on TV, film or in public places. One would think that there would be hymns sung on radio and TV, not godless rock music. One would think we would have righteous laws to protect the unborn.

Yet most people feel that America with her 42 per cent Christian population seems to have a decreasing Christian influence.

Why?

Many profess the name of Jesus Christ, but they are not sincere followers of Christ. In Scripture, when a man became a Christian, he was also a disciple. (follower of Christ) "And the disciples were called Christians first in Antioch" (Acts 11:2). Note, a person had to first give evidence of following Christ before he could wear the label "Christian".

The crying need of the American church is discipleship. Not only do we need to understand the doctrine of discipleship, but we need to practice discipleship.

CONTEMPORARY DEFINITION OF DISCIPLESHIP

But even as some groups are attempting to involve themselves in discipleship, other groups are criticizing them. Why? Because there is much confusion about discipleship. Today there are at least three different ways to define discipleship.

1. *Deeper Life*. Some have felt that the word "Christian" is a misused label because many Christians do not live for Jesus Christ. Therefore, these leaders exhort individuals to more sacrifice, more study, and a deeper walk with Christ. Reacting to "easy believeism", these teach that a few persons can be "discipled" and gain a maturity that is not experienced by the average Christian.

2. *Salvation follow-up*. Some have felt the term discipleship should be applied to new Christians so that they are taught to memorize Scripture, study the Bible, keep a systematic prayer time and witness for Christ. During World War II, the Navigators were an interdenominational organization that emphasized systematic follow-up of new Christians, calling it discipleship.

BECOMING A LEADER

3. *Churching a believer.* Today the term discipleship is coming to mean causing a new Christian to grow in Jesus Christ and incorporating him into the fellowship and service of a local church. This is apparently what the Bible means when it uses the term disciple—a follower of Jesus Christ. Hence, today people are using the term discipleship as the Bible used it.

MAKING DISCIPLES OUR GOAL

The Great Commission commands that we go on to make disciples. The King James is translated, "Go ye therefore and teach all nations". It should be translated "As you are going, make disciples of all nations." (Matt. 28:19). The word *teach* in the original language means "make disciples". The original text is very clear. It says that the task of evangelism is *making disciples.* Nothing short of making disciples fulfills the command of evangelism. As a matter of fact, one author said, "Jesus commands disciple making, not decision making".

The term "discipling" is becoming more popular in this decade. Perhaps it is because we have seen people make empty professions of conversions, but they have not shown evidence of possessing salvation. Since a disciple is a "follower" of Jesus Christ, the emphasis is on more than outward profession but on inward reality. But we should emphasis discipleship not just because the church has superficial Christians, but because it is a biblical mandate. The word *disciple* is one of the most important words in the vocabulary of Jesus Christ.

The word *disciple* occurs 264 times in the King James Bible (occurring only in the four gospels and Acts, but not in the epistles). It is the term that is synonymous with Christian, believer, child of God or son of God. However, Thayers Greek Lexicon lists only five occasions where the Greek verb occurs in the New Testament. The only time "matheuteuo" is used in the imperative (a command) is in the Great Commission Matthew 28:19. The King James uses the word "teach"—which implies to impart instruction. But the imperative of "matheuteuo" implies to make a learner. When the word *teach* is used, it would only imply giving out of the gospel, but the word *disciple* implies both giving out of the gospel and the response of the recipient. To disciple involves a definite commitment by the one who is teaching and the one who is discipled. Hence, the Great Commission wants us to get more than "decisions". It wants us to make "disciples".

Twice the verb "matheteu" is used with Joseph of Arimathaea "who himself had also become a disciple of Jesus" (Mt. 27:57) and "being a disciple of Jesus" (Jn. 19:38). The other two uses of the verb occur in Matthew 13:52 and Acts 14:21.

Therefore, to be discipled means that you have made a commitment to Jesus Christ and you are in the process of following Jesus Christ. Both the initial act (conversion) and the follow-through (sanctification) are implied in being discipled. Hence to be discipled involves the initial act and the

8

continuing experience.

As we look at the doctrine of discipleship, the term was used with at least five different meanings in the New Testament.

CHARACTERISTICS OF DISCIPLES

1. *A disciple is committed to Christ.* Jesus stated that for a person to follow him, he first had to make a commitment—"If any man come to me, and hate not his father, and mother, and wife, and children, and brethren, and sisters, yea, and his own life also, he cannot be my disciple. And whosoever doth not bear his cross, and come after me, cannot be my disciple. So likewise, whosoever he be of you that forsaketh not all that he hath, he cannot be my disciple". (Luke 14:26, 27, 33). At this point Jesus was explaining the initial commitment that a person must make to be his disciple. This is synonymous with salvation, coming to know Jesus Christ as Saviour.

Joseph of Arimathaea is described as "who himself had also become a disciple of Jesus" (Mt. 27:57). The use of the passive tense with the dative implies that Joseph of Arimathaea was discipled into or unto Jesus, but he was not discipled personally by Jesus. Hence, it could better be translated "Joseph, who also himself was Jesus' disciple." Therefore a disciple is one who makes a commitment to follow Jesus Christ. We might point out that many people make such a commitment but do not follow through. In light of the following criteria, we might ask if they are truly a disciple of Christ?

2. *A disciple is committed to the church.* Since the word disciple is used interchangeably with Christian and believer, a disciple must be committed to the church because of a Christian's commitment to the local body of Christ. Acts 2:41 describes that those who gladly received the word were baptized, but they were more than this. They continued daily in doctrine, fellowship, prayers, and as a result "the Lord added to the church such as should be saved." (Acts 2:47) Perhaps the better translation is "The Lord was adding to their number day by day those who were being saved".

Once again this commitment to the local church is seen by disciples, "And upon the first day of the week, when the disciples came together to break bread" (Acts 20:7). Implied in this commitment to the church was attendance because disciples gathered on the first day of the week on a regular basis.

3. *A disciple is committed to the Word of God.* A person who is following Jesus Christ obviously is obeying his commands. Jesus described, "If you abide in my word then are you my disciples indeed" (Jn. 8:31). Jesus gave many commandments concerning personal holiness, practical Christian living and Christian service. Today we have many words such as saturation evangelism, explosion evangelism, coffee house evangelism, personal evangelism, and crusade evangelism. All of these words are "method-oriented", concepts of evangelism which are good and proper. But in the

BECOMING A LEADER

New Testament a true disciple is "goal-oriented" not necessarily method oriented. His consuming passion was to carry out the goals that Jesus Christ gave in the Word of God. Let us always remember as disciples to keep the goals of Jesus Christ in front of us. If we have biblical priorities, methods will take their secondary place. Let us be slow to argue with those who disagree with our methods. Perhaps one believes in saturation evangelism, but someone else practices crusade evangelism. As long as evangelism is getting done, let us praise God for the results.

4. *A disciple is committed to other Christians.* When a person becomes a follower of Jesus Christ, he walks with others on the same road going in the same direction for the same purpose. Jesus says, "By this shall all men know that you are my disciples that you have love one for another". (Jn. 13:35). One of the key words in the New Testament is "together", and since disciples are walking together, working together, and worshipping together; Jesus indicated that a badge of discipleship was love. This is why Luke describes the first manifestation of the church, "And all that believed were together, and had all things common; And sold their possessions and goods, and parted them to all men as every man had need" (Acts 2:44, 45).

5. *A disciple reproduces himself in those who will reproduce others.* The analogy of reproduction is most vividly presented in the parable of the vine and the branches. John 15:1-8. Here Jesus magnifies the necessity of *union* and *communion* with himself, but the purpose is fruitfulness. Christains must be united to Jesus Christ and in constant fellowship with him so that the life of Christ can flow through them to lost people. "Herein is my Father glorified, that ye bear much fruit; so shall ye be my disciples." (Jn. 15:8) The fruit of a disciple is that he reproduce himself by winning others to Jesus Christ and then building up that person by reproducing his life in the new believer.

Even in the heart of the Great Commission is the command to reproduce. Jesus said, "Teaching them to observe all things whatsoever that I have taught you" (Mt. 28:20), and part of the things that Jesus taught us was to grow and make disciples. Hence, a disciple is to go and make other disciples.

LEADERS ARE DISCIPLE-MAKERS

This volume was written to help you become a leader. As such, it was constructed as a resource packet to help someone disciple you into becoming a leader. The title *Discipleship II—Becoming A Leader* reflects its purpose. The following reasons explain why it is necessary to disciple leaders.

1. *Because of the Example of Jesus.* Jesus was God and knew those about him (Jn. 2:25), and he knew his death (Jn. 13:1). Yet he did not invest the majority of his time with the multitudes, although he spent time ministering to the masses. The priority time of Jesus Christ was spent with the men around him, discipling them. If we want to be as influential as

Jesus Christ, we ought to follow his example in discipling others to be leaders.

2. *Because of Spiritual Gifts.* All believers are given gifts. That includes both the one who is being discipled and the one who is training others to be a leader. Yet of all the spiritual gifts that are named in Scripture, there is no gift of leadership. Obviously, everyone who is serving Christ and ministering to others is a leader. Everyone who is a parent is a leader. Everyone who is responsible for another at his employment is a leader.

Since God never gives responsibilities without an accompanying ability, we feel everyone has spiritual gifts (at least embryonically) to fulfill his accountability. Therefore, God has given spiritual gifts to help people become leaders. These gifts can include the enabling gifts of wisdom, knowledge, etc. and the serving gifts such as exhortation, teaching, mercy-showing, etc.

3. *Because of the Command.* The Bible teaches that we are to "produce reproducers", Dawson Trotman's term, who trained men to train other men. The key Scripture, "And the things that thou hast heard of me among many witnesses, the same commit thou to faithful men, who shall be able to teach others also". (II Tim. 2:2) This verse shows that Paul discipled Timothy so that he was able to disciple faithful men. These men in time were able to make disciples of "others also".

4. *Because of the Multiplication principle.* When you make a disciple, you multiply your gifts so that the other person reproduces your ministry into "others also". A person is not discipled until he can communicate that ministry to someone else. Hence, when you make a disciple, you are training someone to be a "reproducer".

The first command in Scripture was God's words to Adam, "Be fruitful and multiply" (Gen. 1:20). The principle of multiplication means "to make many or manifold" or to increase the results by the qualifying number that is put into the process". When we multiply our ministry, we increase the results by what we put into an individual that we are discipling. When we disciple the Word of God and the fruit of the Spirit into him, the result is eternal multiplication.

Jesus illustrated the multiplication of the seed that falls into good ground (Matt. 13:8). Luke describes the church that multiplied in Jerusalem (Acts 6:1), then it multiplied greatly. (Acts 6:7). Finally, he describes the Word of God that multiplies (Acts 12:24).

5. *Because it is cost-effective.* The church can invest its money in many means of evangelism, but that which apparently takes little money but gives great returns is discipling people who will in turn "disciple others also". It is cost effective in terms of money for it costs little. Yet in terms of time, sacrifice, and burden; discipleship costs everything. It is difficult to disciple others, yet if done well, it will last in the ministry of others who will continue to serve Christ.

CHAPTER TWO

THE CHRISTIAN VIEW OF LEADERSHIP*

God has a definite plan for every life. All are to be good followers, faithful servants, and some are to be leaders, themselves led by Christ. All are to ask, Lord, what wilt thou have me to do? Christ, the Master Leader, will direct.

1. *Followship*. Followship precedes leadership. In God's sight it would seem that it is just as important to be a follower as to be a leader, provided we are good followers. We are commanded first of all to "come and follow" Jesus. "Christ's call was to follow him, not to recognize, much less to comprehend him," wrote Sir Wilfred Grenfell in *What Christ Means to Me.*

Christian leadership is only relative. Christ is the only Leader—the rest are humble followers.

"And straightway he called them: and they left their father Zebedee in the boat with the hired servants, and went after him" (Mark 1:20 ASV). "God is faithful, through whom ye were called into the fellowship of his Son Jesus Christ our Lord" (I Cor. 1:9 ASV).

2. *Servantship*. Christ said that if anyone would be great, he must serve. All of those who direct in any phase of Christian work must be servants. Followship and servantship both must precede and accompany Christian leadership. A Christian leader should be thought of as a servant, and should think of himself as such. There should be no need for the term "leadership"; it would be better to say "servantship," for real leaders are truly servants.

This was Christ's attitude. He declared that the "Son of man came not to be ministered unto, but to minister, and to give his life a ransom for many" (Mark 10:45). Therefore, the Christian leader will identify himself with the needs and aspirations of the individuals and the group, and be a servant of Christ along with them in the ranks. Christ said, "Whosoever will be chief among you, let him be your servant" (Matt. 20:27).

3. *Leadership*. Some are called to go further in "followship" and "servantship" and to accept the responsibilities of leadership. Such a task requires faithfulness and ability.

"Leadership," says Dr. John R. Mott, "is the ability to furnish a real lead." It is an art. Leaders forge out into the limitlessness of God's power. True Christian leadership is investing one's life in guiding a group toward worthy Christian ideals and accomplishments; this is service.

---

*Printed by permission, Mary Frances Johnson Preston, from *Christian Leadership* (Nashville: The Sunday School Board of the Southern Baptist Convention, 1934). pg. 3-17

BECOMING A LEADER

Human leadership is needed to carry out Christ's program. People in groups do not always know what to do or how to act; they need leaders. Otherwise no lessons would be taught, no sermons preached, and no Christians trained for the Master's work. Someone must push the work forward and encourage the workers, as well as show the way by staying ahead of the crowd.

"Leadership," says Frank H. Leavell, onetime secretary of Southern Baptist student work, "has surplus of power in reserve, sufficient unto any occasion, and withal can exercise sagacious tact in the releasing of it. Leadership has superior knowledge, but is so skilled in the technique of imparting it, that, like gravitation, silently the power is felt but the source of the power is unseen."

Teaching and training are the two major fields in the educational work of our churches with which Christian leadership concerns itself. "Learning to do by doing" sums up vital principles of the training process in which the leader influences, teaches, and guides. Training includes elements of the teaching process in its strict sense. One cannot be considered entirely apart from the other.

Christ's call is for leaders who can interpret the present situation, but who can also look ahead and plan for the future. His program claims those with positive convictions of things religious, coupled with a willingness to live and act in the light of such beliefs.

No one ever is elected to leadership. Public officials are elected to office, but not necessarily to leadership. An office in itself does not give it; service is its only basis. When the office seeks the leader, it is a wise day. No leader can be made by election. Genuine leadership is the reward of honest, unselfish service that has won the respect and following of the group. Robert E. Lee could go down in defeat, but as one of the most superb leaders the world has ever seen.

II. GOD'S LEADERS OF THE PAST

God's plan of the ages is based upon human leadership under divine commission and guidance. A Christian worker today, serving in ever so small a God-planned place, is in line with his great heroes of the past. God's plan could be traced by a study of his leaders. A mere glance gives sufficient evidence to convince one of such a scriptural basis. Briefly note a few of the many outstanding examples in sacred history.

A deliverer for the children of Israel was needed. God raised up Moses. Moses made excuses and said in effect, "Who am I that I should be entrusted with such great responsibility?" God promised, "I will be with thee." Moses pleaded, "I don't know what to say," and God promised to help him. Again Moses tried to shirk the responsibility by saying, "I am of a slow tongue." Then Aaron was commissioned. But with God as his fellow worker, Moses became a tower of strength and a mighty leader for Jehovah.

When Moses, the man of law and force, and Aaron, the man of religion, were not sufficient for the task of the moment, God gave to Israel a new force—an inspirer—in the person of Miriam. God says, in Micah 6:4, "I sent before thee Moses, Aaron, and Miriam." (Read Ex. 15:1-21.)

Joshua was ready to take his place when it was time for Moses to go.

When Isaiah, in his vision, saw God high and lifted up, he responded to the divine call, "Whom shall I send, and who will go for us?" by saying, "Here am I; send me" (Isa. 6:8). He possessed a spiritual understanding, both of God's will and of his own responsibility. Isaiah's personality was consecrated. "Send me" follows quickly the "Here am I." His response to the divine call and his utter self-sacrifice mark him as a distinguished prophet and leader.

The kingdom needed to be saved from possible destruction, and a woman was ready. Mordecai said to Esther, "Who knoweth whether thou art come to the kingdom for such a time as this?" (Esther 4:14). Queen Esther was God's leader at the right time.

God needed a herald to go before Christ to prepare the way, and John the Baptist appeared. Like a meteor he flashed across the sky and was gone, giving place to one greater than he. John the Baptist was God's man at the time he was needed.

Andrew, the disciple, was usually in the background, but it was he who discovered the lad who had the lunch which Jesus used to feed the multitude. The biggest asset in that crowd around Jesus that day was the lad. It took a quiet leader, who had eyes to see, to discover this lad, and Andrew was that person. The Holy Spirit needed a mouthpiece on the day of Pentecost. Peter, the once hasty, blundering, faltering disciple, was ready, and he preached powerfully. Over three thousands souls were saved that day.

No one in the Scriptures more forcefully and clearly declares the mighty truth of divine commission than Paul, "We are God's fellow-workers" (I Cor. 3:9 ASV). Thoughtful men have been startled by this claim. Some have gone so far as to say that because God is omnipotent, he does not need our help; that God can do anything he wills to do, at any time, with or without our means. While this is true, it does not indicate that we are to sit down and let God do all. The Glorious truth for us is that he wills to use us in accomplishing his purpose.

The Master is the greatest of all leaders, and furnishes the best example and challenge the world has ever known. In his last command (Matt. 28:19-20) Jesus voiced this challenge. Perhaps this Great Commission has sent more soldiers into the frontiers of service than any other single statement in the Bible. Not only is it a great commission, but it is a great permission. "It is the greatest command ever given by the greatest commander to the greatest army concerning the greatest task that the world has ever known."

Coming from the lips of the Saviour, the command has God's approval. It is individual—"Go ye." Christ's ministry was largely personal. His standards are for individuals as well as nations. He called many of his followers one at a time.

His final and last command is a personal command. The command is also powerful, because it has the assurance of God's never-failing word, "Lo, I am with you always" (ASV). It gives us God's plan. It is his outline for the ages—a positive command, a personal challenge, a powerful program. It is possible of obedience, and because of its divine Author should have the pre-eminence. "As my Father hath sent me, even so send I you" (John 20:21).

III. COUNTING THE COST

A Christian leader of the past generation said, "I take hands off as far as my life is concerned; I put thee on the throne in my heart." Gladly did Bill Borden give up his own plans to do the will of the Father. He put himself into God's hands. Self-renunciation and self-dedication are the price of triumphant leadership.

Worth while things cost. There is need to re-emphasize the cost of leadership. Real men do not want "to dream, to drift"—they want dangers to face and loads to lift. Jesus said, "Sell whatsoever thou hast, . . . take up the cross, . . . whosoever shall lose his life for my sake and the gospel's, the same shall save it" (Mark 10:21; 8:35). Thus Christ talked to the people of his generation; he speaks this same message today.

"If you are looking at the price tag and it is too high, then put it down," said a speaker to a group of Christian students. There are many who start out on the pathway of leadership, but when they find that it costs, they forsake the high calling. Sometimes it means that they must change their standards of daily living and lift their ideals. Unwilling to pay this price, they reject the opportunity.

To be a leader does cost, and costs heavily. How?

1. *Losing Self.* Losing life in order to find it, the high cost and unsought reward of leadership. Not saving, hiding, preserving! But losing, abandoning, giving up! The secret of great expansion and growth is the lost life-lost in Christ's cause. The secret of Christian leadership is that at its very heart lies self-sacrifice.

Sir Wilfred Grenfell declares: "Christ ever meant to me a peerless Leader, whose challenge was not to save ourselves, but to lose ourselves; not to understand him, but to have courage to follow him . . . It is obvious that man is himself a traveler; that the purpose of this world is not 'to have and to hold,' but to 'give and to serve.' "

Wheat loses its life to bear new life manifold. The Paradox of living by dying is one of the strangest teachings of Christ. Paul counted all things but loss. Dr. A. Scott Patterson, who lost his health while a missionary in Africa, said: "If the doctors were to tell me I could not get well, I would still want to take the next boat and go back to Africa. Being a missionary isn't a sacrifice. It is a joy. It is a delight. It is a privilege."

Carey forgot himself, and progressed from the cobbler's bench to the mission field. Alice Freeman Palmer, brilliant president of Wellesley College, gave herself freely to those about her, believing that in putting oneself into people, one may go on working forever, as these people touch others, and these others still.

The price of power is the price of giving up. Look about you, and you will see that the leaders who are successful are planting their lives in the lives of others. These have heard and heeded Christ's call to lose self in order to live on. To be a victorious leader one must be willing to give himself up and over entirely, without compromise, to the will of the Father. Jesus taught this long ago.

2. *Finding and Accepting Responsibility.* Accepting heavy responsibility makes the cost of leadership high. It is hard work when a real leader is at the task.

"There is nothing magical about leadership," wrote Mr. Owen D. **Young, "but there are certain penalties attached to it. Men with conscience** and judgment plus courage to act, and willingness to take the penalties of responsibility, are the stuff out of which leaders are made. Ninety-nine out of every hundred men are unwilling to pay the price of leadership and assume responsibility. The road to leadership is not particularly comfortable. You travel it heavy-laden. While the nine to five o'clock worker is lolling at ease you are toiling upward in the night. Forever you are picking up packs that no one else would notice if you left them behind."

Dr. W. J. McGlothlin said: "the sense of obligation was probably the supreme thing in Paul's intellectual and spiritual equipment, and," he continued, "I firmly believe that there is probably no other intellectual and spiritual culture quite so important as the cultivation of the sense of obligation. I would urge every young man and young woman to develop this sense of obligation, of 'oughtness' or 'debt.' "

3. *Knowing Loneliness.* A lonely life may be the price to be paid for leadership. This is not always true, but often it is. When it is the price, it is dear. Said Maeterlinck: "The soul is very lonely. But never is it so lonely as when lifted to a place of shining honor and responsibility. The heights of power are piteously cold. One must leave so much behind when he climbs far above the crowd. In the life of our Lord again and again we catch this note of isolation." If a leader has an idea in advance of the ideas of the group, it is likely to result in loneliness.

It is easy to work hard and give the best of which one is capable when the multitudes are watching and commending and cheering. It is hard to work and sacrifice and labor with a loneliness of soul, and a seeming lack of encouragement or appreciation from some human friend. Remember that God is watching. This magnifies and even glorifies the lonely task—the common routine of a leader's life.

"The only note of complaint I have ever heard from any missionary is, 'I'm lonely!' " said one who has spent forty years on the mission fields. Often a leader stands alone, works alone, thinks alone. Think of Moses, as he tried to lead the children of Israel across the Red Sea. How fickle they seem to have been. They sang his praises one day, and blamed his leadership the next.

Leaders must know that loneliness may come, and must prepare themselves for its pain—"lonely with more than earthly loneliness," as Helen Keller wrote. To a social nature, this is one of the hardest of all disciplines. When the visions are ridiculed, enthusiasm misunderstood, plans rejected by the very persons in whose interest they were made—then the leader is paying the price. The reward and the joy of leadership do not always come, in this life, to those who share its discipline, its pain, and its anguish.

A leader may labor unappreciated, unassisted, fighting almost single-handed, pushing forward the frontiers to make it easier for someone else who is coming. The glorious gleam is that Christ is the comrade. He travels the way, too. That unknown leader who is found faithful Sunday after Sunday, and day after day, even though working in an out-of-the-way place, is paying the price. The reward and final joy and happiness will be great.

Abraham paid the price when he left his homeland, and became the father of a great nation. Joseph paid the price in the pit and dungeon. He remained true to his ideal. Later he saved his family from starvation, and also ruled Egypt. David paid a price in humility, and became a "man after God's own heart." Daniel purposed in his heart not to defile himself, and what an example he furnished today! Paul paid the price on the Damascus road, and all along his eventful life he paid heavy prices to be a powerful missionary leader for Christ. Peter, James, and John left all and followed Christ. Theirs are the name of leaders. Who follows in their train?

When considered from a human standpoint, the price seems great. When seen through the telescope of faith, it seems all too little. To do anything for Christ, who gave all for us is a privilege—not a price!

IV. FINDING A PLACE TO SERVE

Jesus said: "Ye shall be witnesses unto me both in Jerusalem, and in all Judea, and in Samaria, and unto the uttermost part of the earth" (Acts 1:8). "Go ye therefore, and teach all nations" (Matt. 28:19). "Lift up your eyes, and look on the fields; for they are white unto harvest" (John 4:35).

All callings are sacred, for life itself is sacred. For a Christian there is no distinction between the sacred and secular, because Christ is Lord of all. A consecrated schoolteacher is a teacher Christian. First of all he is a Christian, and "teacher" merely tells the kind of Christian. A lawyer Christian or a doctor Christian may be as much a Christian leader as some full-time religious worker.

All are not called to the same task. Some are to be doctors, some teachers, some businessmen, some ministers, some gospel song leaders, some full-time religious workers, some missionaries. Whatever the call and wherever the field—medicine, teaching, business, law, farming, preaching—

all are to be fully Christian, and are to be entered with a sense of divine mission. No matter what vocation pursued, the life should be surrendered to Christ.

From the time Christ said, "Go ye into all the world," there has been work to do. The fields are many and varied. Perhaps each one does not get an opportunity to serve in the place in which he thinks his powers could be most completely realized. God knows best. Is it not wise, then, to consider that "Wherever there is a need, that is a call to let your light shine for Christ."

There are those who have heeded Christ's definite call and challenge, who wish to invest life in kingdom work through his church. A Christian leader will seek to keep his work church-related and Christ-centered. There is no Christian leadership on earth that is worth anything which does not center its program in Christ, and the men and women for whom he died.

If a place of first choice does not open, it may be God's will that the worker serve elsewhere. Paul tried to go into Bithynia to preach the gospel, but the Spirit led toward Macedonia, and thus Europe was opened to receive the gospel. Paul accepted what seemed for the moment to be a second-best choice. As we glance back the nearly two thousand years, it seems to those of us who live today and study his life, that Paul surely did the right and wise thing.

Different talents fit individuals for effective service in different fields. A Christian well may canvass these fields to see where his talents would fit best. Here are some of the questions he may ask himself: Do I work best with adults, with young people, or with children? Where would I be happiest in service? Where is the greatest need, and have I any talent which would make my service there acceptable?

If a person feels no preference for any particular work, he should consider the place, his talents, talk with others, and talk with God about it. There is a place of service for each one, for all are here for a purpose.

If one place of service does not open, then some other should be considered. The door that is open may be God's call. The very circumstances surrounding the open door may be his hand directing into a pathway of duty.

Without exception the leaders who continually achieve most and are happiest in their work are those who possess an abiding sense of the presence of God and an unshakable conviction that he has called them to their task. Theirs are lives with a mission. Leaders under the urge of a divine mission are bound to succeed. God will guide those who are willing to acknowledge the duties right at hand. Those who are in the ranks of duty are prepared to hear the call to go forward.

Near the beautiful Sebago Lake in New England are some wonderful pines that tower high above the rest. Years and years ago, before this land was settled by any but the Indians, King George of England sent men to this country to look for tall trees that would make good masts for his ships. They went up the rivers and lakes, looking everywhere for the special trees. Here on these hills they found these great trees. So the men marked "K.G." on the trees, charted them on a map which they carried, and went on their way. But for some reason they were never cut and carried away to be used on his ships. There they stand today, strong and straight, marked for masts.

"Marked for a mast because they are straight and strong." There are those today who are "marked for a mast," and who will someday fly the colors of a Christian leader. It is wonderful to have been chosen by the King of England and to have been marked for use with his initials, but it is more wonderful to have been chosen by a greater King and marked with his name. Perhaps you can guess what the mark on you might be—it is C.L.—Christian Leader.

"Marked for a mast!" Surely you cannot bend or break if someday you expect to carry a king's colors!

We have only one leader—and that is Christ. The rest are followers—servants. To seek humbly to serve for him challenges one to go beyond the ordinary; to a willingness to pay the price; to deepen one's devotional life through prayer, meditation, and Bible study; to read and study more; to serve better; to live on through the ages by working with real life now; to give Christ the best; to help him have another chance with other lives; to stand at the crossroads in his place; finally, to lose self in Christ's cause. The task cannot be magnified too much. It is a high calling of God in Christ Jesus.

CHAPTER THREE

WHEN IS A LEADER SUCCESSFUL ?

There are certain principles a Christian worker will follow in his work—whether teaching, programming or counseling. These principles are not limited to time or geographical location. They are like the yard stick that one uses to measure. Apply the following principles to see if you measure up to God's standard for success. Apply these principles whether you minister in a suburban church, a youth group, the inner-city mission or the rural church—but by all means apply them.

1. *The leader needs a knowledge of the Word of God.* The leader must know the Word of God and its impact upon lives. This is not a superficial knowledge of Bible content only. He must know the facts of the Bible, but beyond this, he must experience the transforming power of the Word of God in his life. The purpose of the ministry is to produce a change. The Word of God was written to change lives. "For the Word of God is quick, and powerful, and sharper than any two-edged sword, piercing even to the dividing asunder of soul and spirit . . . and is a discerner of thoughts and intents of the heart" (Heb. 4:12). For you to attempt to guide people into a changed life without knowing that change is a case of the blind leading the blind.

You must have a knowledge of the Word of God at your finger tips. The Bible profoundly answers the problems of life. However, the Word of God must be applied. Ignorance causes individuals to treat the Bible as a religious fetish. Many leaders come to the Word of God and quote a Scripture verse as though it had some magical charm. The Bible quoted but not understood cannot be applied to life. Therefore, know the Word of God, its meaning, and apply it to your life. There is no substitute for mastery of the biblical text.

2. *The leader must live by grace a victorious Christian life.* You must know victory over problems. When we speak in terms of the victorious Christian life, we mean victory over something. The Christian has as his foe the world, the flesh, and the devil. All three of these are militantly in opposition to the Christian and would attempt to throw him down. You must know how to diagnose the problems of life. Then you must be able to decide the alternatives to see the sources of power and to apply this power to your own transforming walk of grace. For the leader to have a victorious Christian life, he must have an outlook grounded in firm convictions. Correct behavior comes from correct belief.

3. *The leader must be surrendered to Jesus Christ.* A Christian is a man who has Jesus Christ at the center of his life. This makes Christianity

dynamic rather than static. Becoming a Christian is not simply subscribing to doctrinal statement or giving mere mental assent to the belief of the church. The act of becoming a Christian involves the inviting of Christ into one's heart and life. "But as many as received him, to them gave he power to become the sons of God, even to them that believe on his name" (John 1:12). This makes Christianity alive—Christ lives in the Christian!

Christ desires to control our lives. The leader has two alternatives. He can control his own life, form the alternatives and direct his own future or he he can turn the control of his life over to Jesus Christ This act is called many things. It is yielding, dedicating, surrendering or consecrating your life. All mean the same thing. Yielding involves an act of intellect; the Christian must know God, his Word, and his will. Yielding involves an act of the emotions; the Christian must love God and in love turn all his life over to him. Yielding involves an act of will; there must be a decisive act of the will, whereby the Christian obeys the direction of the Word of God.

If Christianity were to be summed up in one word it would be: relationship—relationship of father and child. We must have a relationship with the Lord, who is the center of our lives.

4. *The leader must counteract the immaturity of followers with the maturity of leadership.* Immaturity produces immaturity. If you as a leader are in spiritual infancy, you cannot expect spiritual adulthood from those who follow you. A leader must possess spiritual maturity at all times, and to have such maturity, he must be mature in the emotional, mental, intellectual, and physical realms. "When I was a child, I spake as a child, I understood as a child, I thought as a child; but when I became a man, I put away childish things" (I Cor. 13:11). Maturity is reflected by your dependability, stability, consistency, and well-rounded life. You will have to be everything the follower is not. You will have to be everything the follower wants to be and should be.

5. *The leader must know the nature of man.* This knowledge is a realization of the dignity and worth of the human being. Christ treated every human being as an individual, created in the image of God. Each personality is similar to others, following the same growth patterns, yet different according to his own environment and heredity. The leader must recognize individual differences and the fact that every person is an individual.

It has been said that people are like breakfast cereal—a surprise in every package. You must realize that everyone has desires, longings, aspirations. But beyond this he has deep-felt needs, problems, and frustrations. These are within the heart of everyone, and you must realize that this person is one for whom Christ died.

Christ, the Master Counselor, could look beyond the face into the heart. He "needed not that any should testify of man: for he knew what was in man" (John 2:25). Christ could see the dignity and worth of the human soul: Because every man is created in the image of God, every man is precious in the sight of God.

You must understand and become interested in every phase of life as it pertains to those to whom you minister. There are two words that are very important. They are:

(a) *Understand.* You must be understanding at all times. With understanding comes acceptance. As a leader, you will be more acceptable and more highly esteemed once you are able to accept each person as an individual—the boy with acne on his face and the girl with the gangling legs; the widow from a poor background and the married couple who lives in an affluent manner. You must understand that each person is trying to adjust to life and trying to find his own place in society.

(b) *Love.* Love is not just an expression of emotion. Love is an attitude and relationship. Just as Christ displayed love to his friends and family, loving them to the end of his earthly ministry, you will have to display love to every one of the persons with whom you come in contact. "This is my commandment, That ye love one another, as I have loved you" (John 15:12).

Just as you must know the Word of God before you can teach the Word of God, so you must know people before you can lead them. The leader must know those to whom he ministers.

6. *The leader must understand the effects of sin.* The Christian community today is quick to name sins, but it fails by not understanding the basic doctrine of sin.

The leader should recognize the total depravity of sin in the individual. When one speaks of total depravity, he does not mean that this person has committed every sin and is lower than the outcast in the gutter. The doctrine of total depravity means that an individual by his own merit cannot stand in the presence of a holy and righteous God. Nothing this individual does can fit him for the presence of God.

The leader needs to know the devastation of sin. Too often we forget that sin has had an effect upon life. The person who sits before us is the "sum total" of every decision he has made. Sin has a cumulative effect. The more one sins, the more hardened one becomes. Therefore, you must realize the nature and cost of sin in the life. A person may give his body over to dope. God will forgive upon repentance, but a psychological effect takes place in the life and physical effects will carry over even after God has forgiven the sin.

The Christian must also realize the subtlety of sin. Many times a person will be telling a counselor what he feels to be the truth, but pride, desire for exaltation, and a lust of the flesh will deceive him. There are times when people do not know their own hearts. Here the leader's duty is to help a person see himself as he really is before God.

The Christian worker must realize the attractiveness of sin. People go through the age of temptation. Never before has sin been made so seemingly attractive. Sin has a great attractiveness to the teenager, but also to adults. Satan will use every tactic possible to pull people away from the will of God. Therefore, the leader will have to understand the effects to better guide followers to victorious Christian living.

7. *The leader must know the nature of our times.* Christians are facing problems they have never faced before. It is the duty of a Christian leader to know the problems, to know the times, and to know people. As people understand what their problems are, what the times are, and what the will of God is; they will better adjust to God's place in life for them.

Some of today's problems are involved with the times. The automobile has given the teenager a radius of fifty miles within a two-hour span. Dating problems are complex. The break-up of the Christian home in our time is unparalleled. The prevalence of divorce, the lack of respect in the Christian home, the excessive emphasis of sex—all give evidence of the character of our times, which is reflected on the magazine racks of most drug stores. These problems confront people, and the leader will have to understand the times to help.

8. *The leader should know the nature of his calling.* If you are going to work with people, you must be many things. Your task is manifold. You are a parent to discipline, a teacher to instruct, a friend to encourage, an employer to supervise, an evangelist to win and a leader to guide.

Your task is supernatural. If God has led you to serve Him, he will give the enabling. Perhaps you think the task is too great. But God's leadership includes his enabling. Your part is to yield to his control and power.

The Christian worker must in a sense be like the Son of God. Christ walked in the midst of publicans and sinners, associated with those who were fallen and looked upon the sin of the world without being associated with the practices of sinful men. The Christian worker must follow this example.

(a) *Christ associated with sinners without sharing their sinful ways.* It is noteworthy that sinners felt comfortable in the presence of Christ. The average worker today makes the unsaved people feel uncomfortable. Christ ate with sinners, fellowshipped with sinners, and they loved to have him around. Is there something about our gospel today that repels rather than attracts the unsaved? Christians have separated themselves from the people of the world when they should have separated themselves from the practices of the world.

(b) *Christ condoned the sinner and condemned the sin.* We see on many occasions that Christ looked past the sin into the heart of the one coming to him for help. The woman taken in adultery was brought and thrown at the feet of Jesus Christ. He did not accuse her; he simply wrote on the ground. Finally Christ asked the woman, "Where are those thine accusers?" Christ accepted the woman, but he did not accept her sin: "Go and sin no more." The Christian worker will have to accept the fact of sin in the life of the people to whom he ministers. Then he must lead the person to forgiveness and to the center of the will of God.

9. *A leader must be able to communicate with people.* The leader must talk the language of those to whom he ministers. This is a basic problem of communication. When a person cannot understand you and you cannot understand him, there is no common point. You will need to understand their "slang" but not use it yourself. Your language must be simple. If you speak above their heads, they may be impressed with your learning. But the aim is to communicate, not impress them.

A leader must break down any barrier between himself and others. Someone else may have constructed the barriers. The person may distrust or not respect the church leadership . They themselves may build the barrier. Nevertheless, the barrier must come down. Communication is making something common to two people. Don't expect them to come to you. When God communicated to man, he became man, took upon himself the form of a servant and came down to human level. In a certain sense you must do likewise.

10. *A leader must be contemporary to the people's time and geared to eternity.* This is another way of saying you should meet the person where he is and lead him to where he should be. God always meets a man where he is, but never leaves him there. God will lift a man to a higher sphere of life if the man is willing. God does not demand that the sinner raise himself to a higher plane before God meets him. Nor does God meet the sinner on a low plane and leave him there. God meets the sinner where he is, and in his sinful condition, then lifts him to where he should be.

Therefore, you should be contemporary to the times. You must understand the longings, desires, and language of people. You cannot stand in the church door and beckon them in. You must go and live in their culture, understanding them, and loving them. Accept people as they are. Present Christ as the one who can help and lead them to a higher level of life.

11. *A leader must establish a meaningful relationship with people.* Most leaders think that they must preach to people. This is far from the truth. People need someone with whom they can have a meaningful relationship of trust, love, and understanding.

A good relationship is the basis of your work. Some leaders make their "flamboyant personality" the basis for their work. These leaders feel sufficient to meet the needs of others. Usually this type of leader has many talents. He can sing, speak, and has a good knowledge of people. When this leader was a teen he had good athletic ability, could carry on a conversation well, and understood life. He feels he can help everyone since he has adjusted well to life.

However, all people are not the same. Times change. Society upgrades itself. Churches become sophisticated. Sin hardens the life. Many factors change people. There is no one leader who can minister to all of the needs of one person, nor is there one leader who can minister to all people.

BECOMING A LEADER

An adequate church program will require a team of workers with different personalities and experiences. Some will be strong in music, others will excel in teaching—then counselors are needed. Finally someone must have the gift of discernment and understanding just to listen to problems and be able to counsel.

But all workers will have to establish a basic relationship with people. This relationship involves accepting them as a person. Too many workers manipulate people. But inwardly, people rebel against being "handled" in such a way. Everyone is a person. A person's best capacities can be brought out in meaningful relationships.

12. *A leader must build independent dependency* in people.* Maturity is growing up, and cutting "mother's apron strings". The mature person is one who does not lean upon others.

The goal of Christian ministry is spiritual maturity. Everyone must be able to stand before God as an individual capable of feeding himself spiritually, serving the Lord, and growing in grace. The spiritual apron strings must be cut from the leader. Then the person should fasten his "loose ends" to Jesus Christ—independent from others—dependent upon God. This is spiritual maturity.

13. *A leader must be church-centered in his ministry.* Christ set up only one institution while on earth: the church. There is no perfect church. As long as it is made up of sinners saved by grace, it will be finite and full of faults. However, "Christ also loved the church, and gave himself for it". (Eph. 5:25)

Build allegiance to the church. There are many independent agencies (youth clubs, Scripture memory programs, camps, etc.) doing good work. But each has a limited contribution. The local church has a continuing ministry.

Even though every church could do better, and most churches have an inadequate program, the local church is the best agency to reaching people. Where would we be if the church had not done the job it has done? Where could we be if the church had done the job it should have done?

Don't permit people to pledge their main allegiance to you. The more they depend on you for spiritual growth, the more difficult it will be for them to stand on their own two feet when you are separated from them. When they move, they will likely falter if they have become overly dependent upon you. A good program will tie people to the local church. They find a stability in being tied to the institution established and blessed by Christ.

---

*This term is used synonymously with maturity.

26

14. *A leader must live an exemplary life before them.* Most people have passed the stage where they will "do as you say but not as you do." Advocating any Christian principle which is not present in your own life is certainly a waste of time and probably more detrimental than helpful.

At the same time do not be a hypocrite. You are not perfect. They will see your faults as well as your spirituality. They must know that you are human with trials and temptations. The Bible does not hide the human faults of men of God. When their shortcomings are viewed, onlookers are encouraged. Just so, others must see your human side as well as your spiritual side. Challenge them to always be striving against sin, running the race, and growing in grace.

15. *A leader must depend on the working of the Spirit of God, not methods.* Remember that such things as motion pictures, panels, debates, slides, and other methods of communication are means to an end, not ends in themselves. Methods can never communicate maturity. The only thing that brings about spirituality is the working of the Spirit in the heart.

Perhaps you will follow a program outline in the manual or teach a lesson that has been successful in past years. Programs, methods, materials, and lesson guides are only instruments used by the Spirit of God. Spiritual growth still comes through the time-honored means. God's leaders must intercede. The Word of God must be applied to the heart. The people of God must dedicate themselves, And the Holy Spirit must do the work.

CONCLUSION

Yours is a great opportunity, but with opportunity comes responsibility. Your responsibility toward every person in your group is to invest your life in him. You must work, lead, and pray that each one may come to a knowledge of Jesus Christ, may grow in grace, and bring praise to the Saviour. With every responsibility that God bestows, there comes accountability. One day you will give an account to God. Determine now that by God's grace you will do your best. Determine that when the Lord comes, he will find you faithful to your important calling, that of working with people.

There are many Christian leaders working successfully with people who have never seen a list of qualifications such as these. They are being used by God because they are doing what God expects of them. A list such as this will not necessarily guarantee success, but will be a guide to a well-rounded leader. If you desire to reach people of your church, make sure that you are living up to the qualifications of a Christian worker.

Check yourself on WHY. Why do you minister? Why do you have the type of program you do? Why do you want to work with people?

Before you read any further, it will help to stop and make a list of the reasons why you want to lead others. Be honest with yourself.

BECOMING A LEADER

Interest in people.

☐ It is an "all right" thing to do.
☐ To keep youth off the streets.
☐ Want to win them to Christ.
☐ To prepare people for church membership.
☐ To have a stronger church.
☐ I like to teach.
☐ Want to take advantage of my training in Christian education.
☐ To teach the Bible.
☐ To develop strong Christ-centered personalities.
☐ To help them find God's will for their lives.
☐ To promote fellowship and recreation in a Christian environment.
☐ To keep people from dropping out of church.
☐ If we don't they go to the "other" church.
☐ Because everyone else is having this kind of program.
☐ To build strong morals.
☐ I have "talents" for working with people.
☐ It's God's will.
☐ People like me.
☐ I'll stay young in this position.
☐ Others:

_____ Total

Score 3 for essential; 2 for good; 1 for irrelevant.
Score: 22-34—limited vision
       35-46—balanced vision
       47 and above—visionary

CHAPTER FOUR

SPIRITUAL QUALIFICATIONS FOR LEADERSHIP*

The life and personality of the leader largely determine the success of an organization or movement. Well-prepared programs are essential; a fine spirit of fellowship warms and attracts others to the group; a carefully kept system of records reveals the progress toward a worthy goal; attractive rooms with comfortable chairs, mounted blackboards, and Bible maps are helpful in solving the problems of leadership; but none of these is the main thing. The leader is the great essential.

There are successful leaders today working in one-room churches and with small groups and limited equipment. This is not ideal, but it is better than having all the equipment that money affords and having the wrong type of leader. Mark Hopkins on the end of a log and a student on the other end was said by James A. Garfield to be his definition of a university.

The responsibility of leadership—whether it be to serve as a full-time religious worker, the director of church training, a Sunday school superintendent, president of some group, teacher of a class, or chairman of a committee or commission, calls for serious and thoughtful consideration before acceptance. Too often people have been urged to accept places of leadership and done so without giving earnest thought to the responsibilities involved.

No doubt many are serving as leaders in one place or another who should not be serving, because of their unfitfulness spiritually or otherwise. Also there are many capable, consecrated, prospective leaders who have not yet been enlisted.

A study of the characteristics of good leaders will be helpful to those who are looking for leaders, as well as to those who are sought for places of leadership. It is essential also to remember God will help those whom he wants for leaders to qualify for the service.

I. RELIGIOUS AND MORAL CHARACTERISTICS

1. *Consecration.* This is a prime requisite of a Christian leader. He must be a consecrated Christian; Christ must have the pre-eminence. His measure of consecration should be perceptible. Consecration is making one's life count for Jesus. It includes wholehearted love for God, wholehearted surrender to Christ as Lord, and wholehearted dependence upon the Holy Spirit as Guide.

---

*Printed by permission, Mary Francis Johnson Preston, from *Christian Leadership* (Nashville: The Sunday School Board of the Southern Baptist Convention, 1934) p. 22-31

BECOMING A LEADER

An outstanding expression of true consecration is the prayer of William Borden, which might be the ideal of a leader today. He said:

Lord Jesus, I take hands off as far as my life is concerned. I put thee on the throne in my heart. Change, cleanse, use me as thou shalt choose. I take the full power of thy Holy Spirit.

Consecration is, in fact, the one great essential in Christian work. Religion is a matter of the heart and life, and the leader's spirituality and his final success depend upon his depth of consecration. It is required in a Christian leader that he seek, first of all, to have the mind of Christ. There should be no doubt as to the sincerity of his religious profession and spiritual qualifications for Christian leadership. Where there is such a question, there is doubt.

An unbeliever or skeptic has no place as a Christian leader. The life should be lost in the will of God. Loyalty to his will makes the true Christian forget self. No one can lead others to find God's will for their lives if he himself is not walking in his will.

"He that doeth the will of God abideth forever . . . " "Thy will be done, as in heaven, so on earth . . . " "As the servants of Christ, doing the will of God from the heart" (I John 2:17; Luke 11:2; Eph. 6:6).

If a Christian brings his will into harmony with the will of the Father, can he not then know, at all times, what God desires of him?

A consecrated leader is one who abides in Christ. Carey was asked, "How is it you've been able to do so much for God?" His sufficient reply was significant: "I don't know, unless it was because God had all there was of me." This is consecration; this is abiding in God's will. Religious truths can be taught, but the religious spirit must be caught.

A consecrated leader is sensitive to God's guidance since all human leadership is only relative. He is also aware of God's hand in directing events in respect to the world and to his own life. He has a realization of the awareness of God. Though he is not to worry over "knowing the times and seasons," a leader may interpret God's workings in his program. Are you afraid to be alone with God? There are some people you would not like to be shut up with. Do you like to be alone in a quiet place with God?

A consecrated leader is a listening leader. God will speak to his servant-leader if he will "hear his voice." Today and in the past, there are and have been those who have dared to listen to his voice rather than the advice of loved ones and friends. They willingly paid with their lives. Their leadership lives on. If Sir Wilfred Grenfell had listened to the voices of friends alone, the Labrador mission work would probably not be open today.

A consecrated leader is one who seeks God, for vital Christian leadership is based upon relationship and surrender to God. Even after becoming a Christian, a person must still seek God, to know his will completely. It seems that people generally expect a little more of a Christian leader—and they should. It is his duty to see that his life meets the added requirements of this second mile of consecration.

We should seek God and seek to live on a high spiritual plane with something of the same intensity that men seek wealth. We get up early, work all day, sidetrack everything that interferes with getting wealth. Is the seeking of God and his will any less intensive than the search for wealth? We should seek God as we seek health. Health gone, and there is no price we would not pay to regain it.

Living daily in the presence of God, we would get another interpretation of things and of the world and a new sense of values; a new conception of tasks involving heavy responsibility and sacrifice.

Consecration reorganizes a life about a new center—Christ. It is not a question of "how much talent" or "how much money," but "how much commitment to Christ." And that is consecration.

2. *Unselfishness.* Of all the places where a selfish spirit is not to be desired, the place of leadership is that one. Here it is required that a real leader have the spirit of Christ, which is the spirit of unselfishness. To prefer others before self, to care not for the glory or the honor that might come, to forget self in rendering service to others for Christ's sake—these are the things which the unselfish person seeks.

Christ said, "He who would come after me" must lose himself. We do not interpret this to mean a wilful, determined resolution. That, in itself, would make it seem a too self-conscious act. But it is rather a voluntary losing oneself in the great cause that engulfs men. Try not to become self-centered, but rather cultivate altruistic ideals and wholesome thoughts.

Livingstone's watchword was "unselfishness." General Booth, sending the one-word cablegram, "Others," to all the posts of the Salvation Army, sounded the keynote of all work for Christ. In the Christian's vocabulary, the word "others" must have a large place. Too many live on the plane of getting all and giving nothing. This is the very heart of selfishness.

At a student retreat each member of the group was asked to tell why he had come. One by one the reasons were given. Some had come to get new ideas, others inspiration, one to get closer companionship with God, another to renew his faith. At the conclusion, the leader of this group of about thirty-five said: "I observe that only one person has come to do anything but 'get.'" One, a bit older, had said: "I came to get all I could, but I have also come to give any help I may from a few years of experience."

3. *Sincerity.* This is a form of honesty. A leader should be sincere and frank both in his own conduct and in his dealings with those he leads. Sincerity is being loyal to the truth in thought, word, and deed, Be willing to admit, "I don't know," but cheerfully respond, "I'll try to find out." It is easy for others to detect insincerity.

The two Latin words "sine cere" mean without wax. In making furniture, wax was used to fill in cracks and other imperfections. Then the cracks were varnished. The furniture looked well. Only usage would reveal the deception. Honest furniture dealers marked their furniture sine cere—

without wax, nothing concealed. So it is with a sincere leader.

If followers have confidence in the sincerity of their leader, they will be seeking him for advice on daily problems, giving him an added opportunity to serve in a much larger capacity than merely directing a program on Sunday. In the long run, honesty will pay the largest dividends.

As a leader thinks of this qualification of sincerity, he hears the echo of an old word, "Whatever is true, whatever is worthy of reverence, whatever is just, whatever is pure, whatever is lovely, whatever is of good repute, if virtue is anything, if honor is anything, be always thinking about these" (Phil. 4:8-9 Montgomery).

4. *High Ideals* A worker for Christ challenges his own soul to be "pressing on the upward way"—to leave the low-vaulted past, to step up to a higher plane, to place his ideals higher.

The artist keeps bright-colored stones nearby so as to keep his sense of color. Even so must the example of Christ ever be the leader's ideal—that his own life may not weaken.

Ideals in the heart count more than in speech. The spiritual success of any group therefore depends on the spirituality, consecration, and ideals of its leader. "Be not conformed . . . but . . . transformed," and the leader must stay close to his ideal, for he cannot lead others close to Christ than he himself is.

The leader possessing high ideals will seek to have the spirit of love ruling his heart. Only these things may a Christian hate: "A proud look, a lying tongue, and hands that shed innocent blood, a heart that deviseth wicked imaginations, feet that be swift in running to mischief, a false witness that speaketh lies, and he that soweth discord among brethren."

5. *Humility.* As Jehovah called his great leaders, it would not seem that he sought those who were anxious for conspicuous places. When Moses was offered the chance to be leader of the Israelites, he shrank from the responsibility, feeling his unworthiness. Through many hard battles he passed—contests with hardhearted Pharaoh and the murmurings of his people—but he leaned upon God and stayed humble.

When the ambitious mother of James and John coveted for them the high places, Jesus replied, "None of you know what you are asking." Then he said, "Whoever among you wishes to be first among you, shall be your slave." In rebuking the high-place hunters at the marriage feast, he said, "For every one who exalts himself shall be humbled, and he who humbles himself shall be exalted" (Matt. 20:22; Matt. 20:26-27; Luke 14:11 Montgomery).

6. *Vision.* Oliver Wendell Holmes divided men into three classes: first, one-story men, who deal with facts and fashions—the scholars; second, two-story men, who deal with theories and ideals—the philosophers; third, the three-story men, who live in the realm of splendid dreams and glorious visions and high ideals—the prophets.

In order to succeed, a leader must have something of this super-sight—to see more in people and situations than others see—to see beyond the difficulties and the present problems to the final successful good and outcome. There are some who can see only self; others who can see beyond self to world needs; and then there are a few who by daily living in the presence of Jesus, and by walking close to him, can see him alone through faith's telescope because self is forgotten in loving concern for Christ's cause.

7. *Faith.* "Without faith it is impossible to be well-pleasing unto him" (Heb. 11:6 ASV). The faith that a leader should possess is the kind of faith that is expressed in Ray Palmer's well-known verse: "My faith looks up to thee . . . Now hear me while I pray . . . O let me from this day be wholly thine . . ." It is a faith that accepts and believes where it cannot prove; a faith that trusts to the limit and that commits the soul to the "blest Saviour".

Great faith can only come from a great soul. No attribute surpasses it. Lifting one out of the dust of despair, it raises to the crags of courageous assurance. By faith the heroes of God's Book conquered. So also will his workers conquer today.

II. EDUCATIONAL AND EXECUTIVE ABILITIES

1. *Mentality.* There are some leaders who possess the qualities of genius, but most of those who are actually doing the work of leadership are those of ordinary ability. In qualifying as a Christian leader, one's mental alertness should be considered. It is not necessary that a leader shine like a star, but he should be a little above the mental level of his group, if possible. He will have to be a bit quicker in thinking, more alert in acting. There are many successful leaders who do not hold college diplomas. They are keeping mentally awake by constant study, by using and therefore increasing the mental powers they have. Education is not limited to school, should it end with a diploma or degree.

A leader should keep on the alert, keep abreast of the times, and keep up with the newest thought in his own line of endeavor by studying general literature and the Bible.

Thorough preparation precedes effective leadership. Teaching a lesson or conducting a program is not easy. Nothing can take the place of special preparation. To appear unprepared is almost certain to result in failure.

Even a small measure of skill, education, or experience would be sufficient to begin with if there be the will to learn. By persistent effort and study, a large measure of each may be acquired. Skills and abilities come as leadership continues. Helpful experience comes by actually leading. Daily the thoughtful leader is developing.

2. *Knowledge of Organization, Methods, and Plans.* Skill in organizing, planning, and directing is a key to success. It comes with practice,

experience, and study. The man with a real experience is the man to fear because he is the man who knows. It was a wise man who said: "Beware of the man with an experience." The methods books give in detail the plans of the various organizations. These plans are workable, and not simply theories someone has imagined. They are results of real experience. These books are valuable. The leader should study each one that has any bearing on his own organization. Every leader must begin by building on the foundation experience he possesses, and then grow by using every available opportunity to increase his ability.

3. *Industry and Resourcefulness.* A leader must be willing to work. There is much to be done. Boys and girls are to be directed in their life choices, programs are to be planned, souls are to be won, tithers to be enlisted, doctrines taught, the Bible to be emphasized, Christ's kingdom to be prayed for. We need Christian leaders who have established right habits of industry.

Jesus worked. He was not afraid of manual labor. As a lad he toiled in Joseph's carpenter shop. One day he closed the doors on the little workshop at Nazareth and went out into a greater work. He quit making tables to go out and proclaim that he was the Bread and life; he went out to say that he was the Light of the world. No more pegs were to be driven, but he was to have the nails put in his own hands; no more earthly houses were to be built, but soon he was to go away to build heavenly mansions. The master Leader of all ages was not afraid of work. He said, "My father worketh hitherto, and I work" (John 5:17).

Ask any successful leader if leading is hard work. The answer is yes. The joy in the task makes the work less irksome, and the happy, industrious leader is the desired combination. The industrious leader who has the other essential qualification of leadership is or becomes the resourceful leader. A place of leadership rarely comes to the person who is not already busily engaged. Resourcefulness increases with application to the task.

With characteristic keenness and industry, Andrew Carnegie, beginning as a bobbin boy in a mill near Pittsburgh, and working from daylight until dark for a dollar a day, foresaw the future of the steel business, and by judicious investment laid the foundation for a future fortune. Right thinking and correct judgement on his part led to right planning and working. These are direct means to personal achievement.

4. *Determination, Will Power, Reliability.* To qualify as a Christian leader, there must be determination to do work in spite of obstacles, the will power to go ahead, make decisions, and the ability to stay by the job. Many fail at this point. Under some inspirational message they determine to give their lives and talents as leaders, and for the first few months all is well. Then will power weakens, worldly pleasures allure, and they fail to stick to the task.

Just when many leaders get to where they could be successful, they resign. Anyone can do that, but it takes a person with real courage and determination to stay, especially when the way is hard. Be sure that it is revealed to you as definitely to resign, as you expect it to be revealed to you to stay on!

Have you seen those who, like the seed sown on stony ground, start out with high hopes, but soon wither under difficulties because they have no foundation upon which to build? Christ, more than any other, refuses to retreat. He accomplished the purpose for which he came into the world.

There is plenty of genius and brillance, but the quality of steadfastness is the rarest of all the virtues. As you rise in the scale of difficult service, you become more dependable. Reliability is a foundation stone of Christian leadership. It is required in a stewart that he be found faithful.

5. *Sound in thinking, Reasoning, Judgement, and Decision.* Thinking is rare enough, but sound thinking is even more rare. So many problems of small moment loom large because of the lack of sound thinking. The ability to think soundly can be developed. Habitually check with care your conclusions in the light of the big aims and the true spirit.

Reason and judgement are added to through the years. Experience gives a clearer reasoning and a truer judgement. Leadership without these basic qualities becomes erratic, inefficient, and ineffective. A leader should reason out problems quietly. The good leader will then add the mature counsel of others to make his judgement the more sure.

CHAPTER FIVE

THE LEADER'S PERSONALITY*

There are phases of leadership which cannot be reduced to rules and principles. A leader may know his program material; he may be thoroughly familiar with the members and their varying needs; he may know how to adapt the program and clinch the thought in his message; he may be in full sympathy with the work; he may even be deeply religious, and still be unsuccessful as a leader. In fact, these things alone will give him no guarantee of success.

An old gentleman tried to teach a Sunday school class of young people for many months before he realized he could not teach. He was a wonderful Christian. He was a Bible student, mature in years and ripe in judgement. He ought to have been a splendid teacher, but he was not. He did not lack culture, education or consecration. He failed for one reason—it was because his *personality was negative*.

The outward tokens of life which we think of as indications of attractive personality are the symbols of something within. Surely the greatest personalities in the world today are made so by the spirit of God.

An attractive personality is essential for successful leadership. It is therefore desireable, in studying self, to study elements of attractive personality.

I. WHAT CONSTITUTES ATTRACTIVE PERSONALITY

Personality is defined as that which constitutes a person. It includes every attribute—emotional, mental, physical, and spiritual. Personality is also that which differentiates. It is an intangible quality about one that makes him different from other people. It is a mysterious magnetism that either draws people or repels them. It has a powerful influence, and is far-reaching in its results either for good or evil.

Personality is character plus; it adds to character the ability to reproduce itself in others. There are people with fine Christian character, but poor expression of personality. Personality is that thing about a leader which projects to the back row of a group, and holds the attention of the most inattentive member.

What, then, contributes to personality to make it attractive? Good habits, cleanliness in thought, words, acts and conduct, daily living. The outward manifestations speak of something within. Reading good books, associating with strong personalities reflect favorably on one's own. No doubt, some traits are inherited; many are acquired. Magnetic personality

*Reprinted by permission, Mary Francis Johnson Preston, from *Christian Leadership* (Nashville: The Sunday School Board of the Southern Baptist Convention, 1934) p. 42-52

depends more on good health, mental awareness, and spiritual qualities than on physical beauty.

As these qualities of attractive personality are studied, each one will make the application for himself.

1. *Sympathy and Ability to Understand.* Of all the qualities which go to make up the personality of a leader, none is more important than sympathy. A leader should cultivate a mental attitude of giving himself to others. If a boy knows his leader is sympathetic and has an understanding of him and his problems, he unconsciously is drawn toward his leader, admires him, follows him, and co-operates with him. He needs to know that there is someone counting on him! This factor in itself is a powerful influence.

A comprehending leader possesses the key that inspires the confidence of others and opens pathways into the hearts of his members. He understands the background of the people with whom he works. He understands their outlook. One who can remember well enough to live again in that world of yesterdays when he himself was the age of the group he leads, will find easy access into the lives of his members today.

A tight handclasp or a "That's fine" smile often reveals an understanding heart, and they go further than mere words. Jesus, more than anyone else, could understand, sympathize, and love in spite of apparent faults and circumstances. A love for people will finally result in a love of people.

Almost imperative is the need for leaders who possess this valued gift of appreciating and understanding people. With many this ability is a gift. With any who lead, it must be developed if the leadership is to exert far-reaching influence. It may be developed through contacts with people, through retrospection, and by living with and loving people.

2. *Self-Respect as Expressed in Personal Appearance.* The leader should strive to be neat and attractive in personal appearance. The power of example is so great, and the influence over others is so strong, that one cannot afford to appear at less than his best every time he meets his group. There is nothing wrong in a moderate amount of time spent on one's personal appearance. It is commendable. There is something stimulating and refreshing about a person who looks his best. It involves self-respect and encourages confidence. Correct personal habits have a remarkably wholesome effect on others. Therefore, a leader should appear at his best always.

"Better looking teachers mean better discipline and better teaching," said an educator in an address to a teachers' convention. A good looking leader is one who is attractive, no matter what his features may be. A leader who takes pains to be neat and bright and cheerful has a decided advantage over one who neglects his personal appearance.

Clothes may not make the man, but their choice and the way they are worn reflect the inner man.

3. *Cordiality and Friendliness.* "With what measure ye mete, it shall be

measured to you again" (Matt. 7:2). If the leader expects others to warm up to him, he must lead the way. A genial spirit lends warmth to a meeting and encourages fellowship. People will go where they are welcome. The leader should cultivate a smile and a hearty handclasp. A cordial spirit is catching; it spreads. Let the leader set the pace for the group in seeing that a spirit of cordiality prevails. A cordial handshake and a hearty greeting are welcomed by members and visitors at all times. Nobody warms up to icebergs.

Wherein do your riches lie? A prominent religious leader says, "I'd rather be rich in friends than in money." He is a man of a million smiles and nearly as many friends. His radiant personality always gets a response.

4. *Tact*. Tact is knowing what to do and say at the right time, and how to do and say it, and doing it and saying it. Tact is an attitude plus action. It is based upon an appreciation of the other person's position. This ability to put oneself in another's place and to appreciate his point of view is especially valuable in a leader. It is a native gift with many people, but it is a quality which can be cultivated.

Tact involves precision, poise, firmness, reasonableness, and a sense of humor. These qualities should be combined in a leader's personality. If not there by native endowment, they should be developed. The tactful leader is the co-operative leader. Being tactful, yet firm, strong, and absolutely fair, will receive as its response true loyalty on the part of the group to the leader.

5. *Optimism, Enthusiasm, and Courage*. Optimism helps to overcome difficulties. Can an obstacle defeat the leader as long as he has optimism and hope? Difficulties test the outlook of a leader. They have given many the chance of their lives. Consider Carey in India, Judson in Burma, Lottie Moon in China, Florence Nightingale in the Crimean War, and Frances Willart in the backwoods of Wisconsin. Helen Keller, blind, deaf, and dumb, overcame three severe handicaps.

As the oyster changes the irritating grain of sand into a pearl, so does the man of optimism turn difficulties into stepping stones of achievement. A damp, dark dungeon has housed many a leader who still was able to lead. John Bunyan sends out his *Pilgrim's Progress* from Bedford jail. Luther translates the Bible while confined in the Castle of Wartburg. Paul, in his cell in Rome, gives us Philippians, the loveliest and most joyful of his epistles. He had his thorn in the flesh, though he never told us what it was, and he didn't complain about it every time he wrote a letter. Beethoven was deaf when he produced his greatest musical composition. Milton was blind, poor, and sick, but he sent this message of hope out to the world in one of his finest sonnets, "They also serve who only stand and wait."

David Livingstone could have been found working in a little cotton factory at the age of ten. At fifteen years Edison was a newsboy on a train. At twenty-five years Carey was cobbling shoes to support a family. "When I found I was black," said Alexander Dumas, "I was determined to live so that men would be forced to look below my skin." John Wanamaker's first job in a book store brought him only $1.25 per week, and he used to walk four miles daily to the city.

The leader's optimism is not a false philosophy of "positive mental attitude", but a vital and real faith in Christ to overcome. Where worry kills and depresses, hope and optimism will uplift.

Experience proves the truth that whatever is worth doing at all is worth doing with enthusiasm. Enthusiasm is contagious, for the leader's enthusiasm will kindle a like enthusiasm in the minds of his members. When Paul wrote Romans 12:11, he said, "Be glowing in spirit." Dr. Moffatt translated it: "Maintain the spiritual glow." Enthusiasm is a protective power in a leader's own heart against discouragement. It indicates a dominant passion which so masters his spirit that he believes he can do the impossible, and often he does it, proving that an "impossibility is an impossibility." Enthusiasm admits no failure!

A courageous leadership is needed. Some violent breaks with conventionalities may be necessary. Lonely ventures and difficulties are in store for the courageous leader. Courage comes from a sense of the presence of God. Can a man be discouraged when he has this sense of the Presence with him? Mary, Queen of Scots, is said to have dreaded the prayers of John Knox more than all the armies because she knew his courage and faith.

Should a leader allow his members to know when he is discouraged? Times of depression will come, but the courageous leader will seek to rise above them. The spirit of optimism, enthusiasm, and courage will overcome many handicaps.

Consider these three suggestions for the discouraged leader. *Look in* and see if the trouble is within your own being. Correct it. Maybe your prayer should be, "Create in me a clean heart, . . . and renew a right spirit within me."

Look out and command help. Perhaps one assistant would lighten the load and remove the discouragement. Seek mature counsel from one who knows the Lord.

Look up to Jesus. He knows how you feel. Remember his promise to be with you all the way. "My God shall supply every need of yours according to his riches in glory in Christ Jesus" (Phil. 4-19 ASV). "My grace is sufficient for thee: for my power is made perfect in weakness" (II Cor. 12:9 ASV). Should not a leader face his perplexities in the assurance that God is with him?

"When Abraham Lincoln was a young man, he ran for the Legislature in Illinois and was badly swamped. He next entered business, failed, and spent seventeen years of his life paying up the debts of a worthless partner. **He was in love with a beautiful young woman, to whom he became** engaged, then she died. He then tried to get appointment to the United States Land Office, but failed. Entering politics again, he ran for Congress **and was badly defeated. He became a candidate for the United States**

Senate, and was defeated in 1858 by Douglas. One failure after another, bad failures, great setbacks. In the face of all this, he eventually became one of the country's greatest men, if not the greatest. When you think of a series of setbacks like this, doesn't it make you feel small to become discouraged just because you think you are having a hard time in life?"

6. *Vitality and Vivacity.* Here is a blending of physical stamina and mental alertness. Energy accompanies these, too. They never fail to make a good impression. The channels of their expression are the voice, well modulated, clear, convincing, and the eyes and the quickness in movement of the body. Physical fitness fills an important place in a leader's personality. One cannot be or do his best under physical handicaps.

Grenfell gives health an important place when he says that "Christ to me is the justification and inspiration to keep my body and mind fit and perfect, that thereby I may preserve myself, my soul, fit to accomplish, able to serve, and confident that I shall hear over there, not 'You are loosed from the wheel of life, you can now enjoy forgetfulness,' but, 'Well done; here are more talents for you, and more victories to win.'"

Health is a prime requisite. Leaders should realize this and arrange for rest periods, for sufficient sleep, exercise, recreation, any of the things necessary to make them alert, attractive, physically able to carry on. Everyone admires a strong man. These types appeal to youth especially. Athletic leaders are often the great heroes, not only of boys and girls, but adults. Good health is necessary for the most successful leadership, and for a wholesome influence on the membership of the group.

The other side of the question should be emphasized also. Perhaps there are steps to be taken to overcome physical handicaps. Strength may be added by a few more hours of rest at night or by living and working as much as possible out of doors. Consider many great leaders who were physical weaklings, and overcame. No doubt the world has lost many who could have been leaders because they did not know how to overcome their physical handicaps.

The three essentials for proper living, apart from the moral aspects, are (1) correct exercise, (2) sound sleep, (3) good food. Without these the blue Mondays come too often, lines of pessimism come into the face, and soon the once acceptable leader becomes nervous and irritable and wholly undesirable. A person of this disposition has no right to be leading youth.

The study of health and how to keep well should be given careful consideration by everyone. One's body is the gift of God and should be kept as such. We should read, study, and practice principles of correct physical living.

7. *Thoroughness, Artistry, Earnestness.* Artists are needed in leadership work; those who give attention to detail, workers who finish the job. No man with a sense of God could fail to do his finest work even on the smallest detail.

8. *Kindness, Courtesy, Consideration.* These are three in one. The person who possesses a lovable disposition will show forth these characteristics to a marked degree. Can a person be considerate without being kind? Or courteous if not considerate? How they are entwined together! The kind leader never drives, but encourages; the courteous leader practices the Golden Rule, and the considerate leader is ever thoughtful of others. These three are the very essence of unselfishness.

9. *Poise, Patience, Tolerance, Self-Control.* Could a more important group of desirable traits be mentioned? Each of these is related to the other. In some measure they are interdependent. Some persons have poise; others need to work and concentrate to attain it. Patience is greatly desired. Willingness to make haste slowly is a lesson many need to learn. Do leaders pray for patience, and then when a chance comes to exercise it fail to respond? The leader who exercises tolerance will respect the opinions and beliefs of others. He will co-operate in a common good even with those with whom he differs. A leader must exercise self-control and restraint. Many times the respect and following of the group depend upon these.

10. *Sense of Humor.* This will save many a situation. A leader should be firm when necessary, but acquire and use a sense of humor. Over and over the display of this admirable quality will win friends for the leader and the cause he represents. It will help to ease tense situations.

11. *Regularity and Promptness.* The regularity with which one meets his obligations and engagements is an index to his character. Regularity and promptness indicate a wholesome respect for the rights of others. A leader may not expect his members to be regular if he himself is not. If week-end trips allure him to other places, he must not expect his members to be more loyal than he. To be prompt, be present ahead of time. Perhaps ten minutes ahead of time is "on time" for the leader.

12. *Originality and Initiative.* These are gifts. Some have ears keener to hear, eyes quicker to see, and greater capacities to conceive new ideas and new arrangements of ideas, than others. If a leader is fortunate enough to be so resourceful, thrice blessed is he.

13. *A Spirit of Co-operation.* Willing and cheerful co-operation cannot be overlooked, for the leader who has not learned how to co-operate will find himself developing a rebellious spirit and his leadership will suffer. Willing co-operation from others comes always in response to wholehearted co-operation already given them by the leader.

14. *Self-Confidence and God-Reliance.* The right sort of self-confidence will not be egotistic, but will rely wholly upon God who gives strength. Paul was self-confident, but he was God-reliant also, especially when he wrote, "I can do all things through Christ which strengtheneth me" (Phil. 4:13). We are expected to have the victory; it requires confidence in one's ability, but also an entire leaning upon the Holy Spirit.

CHAPTER SIX

JESUS CHRIST—THE IDEAL LEADER*

Jesus was the ideal leader. He willingly spent thirty years training for three years' work. How significant that is, for most of us would wish to reverse the order. This very fact in his own life gives keen insight into our preparation for leadership. Are we seeking to enter upon a life task before the period of preparation is over. Christ paid the price in preparation.

Christ knew the Old Testament, and often quoted it. But scholarship was not the final interest of his full life. He kept in close touch with the members of the group he led. Religious knowledge was not forced into him by books, but rather came forth from his heart because of experience with the Father. In his own heart he exercised the most wonderful faith the world has known anything about.

He spent his leadership hours living with others—touching their lives, eating with them, talking with them, teaching them, and lighting up the ways of life for them. What a Saviour Jesus is! Yes, and what a leader! Tempted in all points as we are, criticized as leaders are. Yet in him we see all that a leader should be and can ever hope to be. He is "Our All in All."

JESUS, THE LEADER

When Jesus began his earthly ministry he was confronted with the mighty task of training his 12 disciples within the period of three short years. What method will he use? What kind of organization will he build?

If he had left his plan of organization to me, I would have arranged his itinerary in such a way as to bring him in touch with the greatest number of people. I would have gone before him making engagements in the largest cities and building enormous tabernacles to accommodate thousands of people in order that he might have the greatest possible hearing for his message.

Jesus had better sense. That is why he did not turn the task over to me. He adopted an entirely different method. He assembled an intimate group, believing that this would be the quickest, shortest, and most permanent plan for the accomplishment of his purpose. Choosing a little group of disciples who had pledged their love and loyalty to him, he quietly began his work of training. If he placed this high valuation upon training, it will richly repay us to study his method.

---

*Reprinted by permission, Mary Francis Johnson Preston, for *Christian Leadership* (Nashville: The Sunday School Board of the Southern Baptist Convention, 1934) p. 33-38.

BECOMING A LEADER

1. *Jesus' Program of Training.* Let us notice first his program of train-ing, that we may be able to follow his example. He realized that there were at least four elements which must enter a well-rounded plan of Christian development; namely, devotional, Bible study, doctrinal, and missionary. He used these four types of resources in training his group.

Since it was a spiritual task to which he was calling these twelve, he arranged certain meetings for the development of their devotional life. Sometimes they would sit together on the shores of the Sea of Galilee or come apart 'into the mountain alone,' and there he would talk to them about the deep things of the spirit, prayer, communion with the Father, personal consecration, and the leadership of the Holy Spirit.

Since his message had a direct relation to that of the Old Testament writers, he realized that these young Christians must have a place in their programs for Bible study, so we find him unfolding the Scriptures to them, interpreting the law of Moses, explaining the messages of the prophets, reviewing the history of God's leadership of Israel.

If they were to become great preachers and teachers, he must also teach doctrine. Thus he expounds the great doctrines of sin, repentance, regener-ation, sanctification, the justice, mercy, and love of God.

The message taught by Jesus is a message for all the world, so the disciples must be trained in missionary work. We are not surprised then to find the leader devoting whole programs to study mission, telling the young disciples that they are to be his witnesses 'in Judaea, and in Samaria, and unto the uttermost part of the earth,' that they are to 'go . . . (into all the world) and make disciples of all the nations, baptizing them into the name of the Father and of the Son and of the Holy Spirit' (ASV).

2. *Problems Which Jesus Faced.* Jesus found himself confronted with great problems as he undertook the difficult task of training recruits. If this were not so we would find little profit in studying his plan of work, for we have discovered that our organizations have to wrestle sometimes with problems. The problems of this group were not essentially unlike those which we meet today.

(1) The foremost problem was that of the leader's own personal temp-tation. He was called upon to meet the great Adversary and to feel the power of his temptation. It was not the lure of gross and revolting sin, but the more insidious temptation to lower his standards, to turn aside from his appointed task, to avoid the cross, to find some easier path. Satan tried to persuade Jesus to use his miraculous power to provide bread, which would make a selfish appeal to great throngs of people to enlist in his cause. Failing here, he next proposed a spectacular display of power which would startle the people into acceptance of his claim of kingship. The final offer was a compromise with the evil one which would do away with the neces-sity for the sacrifice of Calvary. In each case, the temptation was to avoid the terrible sacrifice which in the plan of Jesus was the foundation for enduring success. Is that not our temptation today, the temptation to

escape sacrifice, to avoid hard work, to find some short cut?

(2) The critics were alive in Jesus' time as they are today. They constitute one of his most aggravating problems. Wherever Jesus turned, he confronted the scribes and Pharisees, who criticized him at every point and found fault with everything that he did. His unfailing patience should be an example to us when we find our purposes questioned and when we find ourselves criticized by pastors, deacons, or church members who are harsh and unreasonable in the demands which they make upon us.

(3) Ignorance was another problem. Jesus found the members of his group slow to learn. Sometimes when his heart was all aglow with enthusiasm, and when he was teeming with great plans, he found his followers dull and ignorant. Even as he neared the close of his ministry, he was shocked to hear them asking about an earthly kingdom, disputing with petty jealousy over the distribution of honors. James and John both wanted to be secretary of state and Judas wanted to be secretary of the treasury. In infinite patience Jesus dealt with their ignorance. Beginning at the first, he taught them all over again, and seemed never to grow tired in the task.

(4) In the garden of Gethsemane Jesus met the baffling problem of weariness in the members of his group, who calmly slept while he prayed and sweated blood. Sometimes today when a leader puts his very life into some ambitious plan trying to stir up interest among his members; he discovers to his dismay that they are asleep, apparently indifferent and altogether unconcerned about the work of God. What is a leader to do under such circumstances? Do just what Jesus did, wake them up.

(5) The great crushing problem of the group came when Peter sinned. Here was a problem indeed. Peter, the most prominent member of the group, the man whom everybody knew to be a member, the one who talked the most and made the loudest profession; had fallen into disgraceful sin. His sin was committed right in the presence of the enemies. He brought disgrace upon himself and upon the group. What was the leader to do? Forgive him.

Jesus here exhibited the highest type of leadership. He turned and looked at Peter, and with that one look broke the heart of the erring disciple. It was that look which finally led to his repentance. If you as a leader can come to know your members, and enter into their experience and life, you can have a position of influence on them. You will demonstrate that you have learned the great lesson of Jesus' leadership.

3. *Dealing with Individuals.* All great training deals with the individual. Notice Jesus' method with the various individuals in his group. Here is Judas, a member who never did have any genuine interest. His name is on the roll, but he has no spiritual fellowship with the group. Jesus shows his greatness of heart in his treatment of Judas; anxious to give him a fair chance, Jesus gives to him a place of responsibility and honor, and makes him the treasurer of the little company. He yearns over him, prays for him,

gives him every opportunity for repentance and salvation.

Peter, James, and John constitute a group which must be handled in a different manner from the others. They are stronger, more aggressive, and further advanced than the others. Jesus did not hold them back, but gave them special opportunities for service and development. On several occasions we find him leaving the rest of the group and taking these three with him. They are with him on the Mount of Transfiguration; they are permitted to witness the raising of Jairus' daughter; they go further with him into the experience of Gethsemane.

The wise leader will provide tasks suited to the needs of individuals, and will recognize the fact that certain members have greater capacities and possibilities than others.

But Simon Peter must be considered even apart from the other two. He is a problem all by himself. In fact, he positively refused to be like anybody else. He represents the type of member who is inclined to monopolize. When they put on a program, he always speaks overtime. Sometimes he blurts right out in the midst of another's speech. Then again he insists on speaking even when his group does not have charge of the program. Jesus displays fine sense of judgment in dealing with him. Recognizing unusual possibilities in Peter, Jesus does not crush his spirit, but does sometimes give a needed rebuke. His blundering speech on the Mount of Transfiguration, his untimely advice to Jesus about going to Jerusalem, his rash impetuosity in cutting off the servant's ear, all these things tried Jesus sorely. But the great Leader never lost his patience with Peter.

Andrew was an individual of quite opposite type from his brother. He represents the member who does not like to be in the public. When they would assign him a part on the program, he was sure to be absent. What is the leader to do with such a member? Would it not be wise to give him up and drop his name from the roll? Jesus adopts a wiser plan. He finds the thing for which Andrew is especially fitted, and assigns that task to him. He makes Andrew chairman of the membership committee. There he renders a mighty service and achieves undying fame, for it is during his chairmanship that the membership committee enlists Simon Peter, the strongest member of the whole group. On the day of Pentecost, when Peter preached the great sermon and three thousand people were converted, there must have been somewhere in the throng a quiet, unnoticed man who listened with tears in his eyes and said to himself, 'I introduced that man to Jesus.'

4. *Our Inspiration.* The group which Jesus led is our inspiration and our example. A program of training with its emphasis upon devotional life, Bible study, doctrinal teaching, and missionary activity is copied directly from his plan. The problems of this group are the problems which we meet today. We shall be able to solve these problems only as we learn of him.

CONCLUSION

Every leader obviously does not embody all of the qualifications discussed in this book. Taken together, they would probably make the ideal leader. We do have such a person in Christ Jesus.

Nevertheless, one should not hold back because of a sense of unfitness. He should start with the qualifications he has, and work and pray, discipline himself persistently. Soon his personal equipment will improve. It is encouraging to know that a leader is not static, but grows under responsibilities.

A leader must maintain high personal standards; go about the work with a steadfastness of purpose; be conscientious in the performance of duty. After days, and months, and perhaps years, there will come a degree of difference. This degree will be the advance over the old self.

Leaders are not all necessarily "born leaders"; they can be made. Unless one possesses definitely some quality that would entirely disqualify him, then by persistent effort, faithful study, and prayerful work, he can learn. This should be a gleam of hope for many who may now be discouraged. From year to year you will be growing, even as you are helping others to grow, and as you are helping to carry out the mission Christ gave when he said, "Come ye" and "follow me" and "go ye."

CHAPTER SEVEN

UNDERSTANDING THE NATURE OF MINISTRY

What then is our spiritual ministry to which we give our leadership? *To relate the gospel to persons at the point of need.* Carroll Wise has given the following definition of pastoral care: "We have defined pastoral care as the communication of the gospel to persons at the point of their need."[1] This definition will be exanded from the scope of the pastor to include a ministry that can be performed by any leader in the church. This is spiritual ministry whether on a "one-on-one encounter," a lecture or leading a group over an extended time. We shall divide our definition of ministry into three sections. The last part of the definition is dealt with first: the point of need. Second, we shall deal with relationships—a path to maturity. Third, we shall attempt to answer the question, "What is the gospel?"[2]

1. *Ministry—to the point of need.* All ministry begins with God and has its eternal existence in God, but there was no need of ministry until God created man. As soon as man was created, a need existed. Man was made in the image of God, which means among other things that he had the ability to reason. His intellectual ability reflects the thought processes of God. Man also had emotions, as expressed in the feelings of love and hate, to mention just two. Finally, man was a volitional being who could decide his own fate. So, when Satan came and tempted, "Ye shall be as gods," man, who had the ability to make a moral choice, fell into sin. Sin produced the greatest need in man and ministry is the channel through which God would meet that need.

Man is cut off from God. Not only Adam and Eve, but everyone from that time forth was excluded from God's presence. The Scriptures teach, "For all have sinned and come short of the glory of God" (Rom. 3:23). This included every child who was born in the line of Adam and Eve, since "as by one man sin entered into the world, and death by sin; . . . so death passed upon all men, for all have sinned" (Rom. 5:12).

Man's sin is classified into three aspects. First, anything less than God's perfect holiness is sin. Sin is similar to an arrow falling short of the target. It did not attain to the perfect standard. So every person born into the world does not measure up to God's perfect standard.

Rebellion is the second aspect of sin, usually translated "transgression." Sin is the breaking of God's law, either volitionally or ignorantly. God prohibits the worship of idols, but man sins when he falls upon his face and worships a wooden statue. He has transgressed God's commandment.

The third aspect of sin is inherent wickedness or moral impurity. This is described as filth or uncleanness and is abhorred by God, who is pure and holy.

The result of sin is that it blinds the sinner (2 Cor. 4:3, 4; Eph. 4:17). Usually man does not recognize that he is a sinner and that he is cut off from God. Therefore a sinner needs the gospel communicated to him at his point of need, to reveal to him that he is a sinner.

Man becomes his own point of reference. When Satan promised Eve, "Ye shall be as gods" (Gen. 3:5), he fulfilled that promise. As a result, each man today is his own standard of measurement. Each has become the focus of the circle in which he lives. A wise man once observed, "There is some divinity in us all." By that he meant that each man justifies his own actions and thinks that everything he does is perfect or at least almost perfect.

The Fall of man has created an upside-down condition. Instead of man's placing God on the throne, man sits there in supreme ignorance that he has usurped the place of God. Doctrine teaches man that God must be placed on the throne and only when man understands God's nature and program can man begin to get his problem solved.

Man suffers alienation and isolation. Too often people think that sin is punished after death. That is only part of the picture. People suffer the consequences of sin in this life. Sin results in isolation or alienation from God. Spiritual death is the ultimate form of isolation from God. As a result of man's sin, he needs eternal salvation to bring him into fellowship with God. But there is a second problem. Modern education speaks of "felt needs," those problems we are aware of, and "ultimate needs," usually the problems that are real but unexperienced. The "ultimate need" is salvation for man to be rejoined to God from whom he was cut off. But let us not forget the "felt need," the deliverance from the affliction in this life that also springs from our sin.

Isolation from God may not be a felt need, but severe depression is an experience that needs immediate help. To this person, the doctrinal message of fellowship with God may not be enough, but it is the foundation of all ministry to that person. Since man is a social creature, his problem of isolation may be the root of many of his other mental or psychological problems.

The answer to isolation is that God took the initiative with man. **"When the fullness of time was come, God sent forth his Son"** (Gal. 4:4). And again we read "God . . . hath in these last days spoken unto us by his Son" (Heb. 1:1, 2).

Man is filled with anxiety. Any life that is separated from ultimate authority is like a boat without an anchor: it is drifting. A person may be anxious because he does not have all the answers to the questions raised by others or even the questions asked in his heart.

Every person has within his heart a need, something missing that only God can fill. He knows that something is missing but he usually refuses to identify it as God. He looks for answers elsewhere and does not find any. He becomes his own point of reference, but he makes mistakes and is aware of his own stupidity.

People are anxious because they have a problem keeping their emotional lives together. God should function in man's immaterial nature, but the vacuum created by his absence produces anxiety. "Anxiety" is another word for fear, depression, jealousy or any other condition that keeps man in an emotional disequilibrium.

Man searches for meaning. Because man is isolated and affected by sin in every part of his life, the lack of meaning in life becomes a felt need. Those who are slaves to drugs know that narcotics do not lead to happiness or meaning. The same can be said for wealth, fame or even success.

Some people do not know where to go or how to get where they want to go. But they want to go somewhere. They are like a fine-tuned car that has a full tank of fuel but is without direction or purpose. Others are bewitched or have dropped out of the human race. They have no drive or no desire. They are like a car without fuel, without a battery, and with a rusting engine. Both have problems with meaning—they have not found the secret in life. They need the revelation of God that gives the purpose for which men should live.

Man marches inevitably toward death. We are frightened when we see a young friend struck down with cancer, and yet thousands die annually of some form of cancer. We experience the same fear when a child is killed or we hear of a young son who is missing in war.

The threat of death is all about us. Then we look within our decaying bodies and realize death is our enemy. We are spirits that want to rise above the limitations of the body. Yet we see dimly because our eyes are wearing out. Our arms ache because of arthritis. Even the thirty-year old feels the inevitable rising tide of age when a younger man takes his place on the team.

The Bible teaches that "the wages of sin is death" (Rom. 6:23), and the ultimate need of man is an explanation for death. A little boy was standing next to his father on the front seat of their Mercedes Benz. The father had given his son everything. Then the little boy asked, "Does everyone have to die? The father thought a moment then answered, "Yes," The young son pondered that answer, then blurted out, "Even if they are lucky?"

The basic application of sin in a life is felt in isolation. As a teen moves from the world of adolescence and high school into the world of the young single adult, a radical transition takes place. High school was filled with clubs, activities, and home rooms. High school was a place of many friendships. But now, the young single adult is cut off from many relationships. In the large impersonal city, people are reduced to digits on a computer. The young single adult by his very nature "unattached" lacks deep meaning from relationships that build healthy personalities. Separation can lead to a disassociated personality. The fractured personality is not whole or complete, and the whole or healthy person is called mature. The isolated person is a potential drop-out to the church.

The adolescent faces the conflict of identity. His parents want him to go to college. The boys with whom he buddies want him to join the army. His steady girl may want him to drop out of school and get married. The adolescent calls a moratorium (a period of time when he puts off making decisions). In young single adulthood, the moratorium is over and a young person must face the problem of identity, Who am I? What shall I be in life?

As the young single adult struggles with the problem of self-identity he feels, "I am a face in search of an identity." This search may cause the young adult to be unsure of himself and insecure in group gatherings. Many times he feels a wall between himself and other lives. He feels alone or isolated. This psychological need is evident, but man has a deeper need—spiritual.

In developing spiritual ministry, conversation is important, but the relationship that undergirds the conversation is more important. Never depend on the magic of words. Just because the right thing is said at the right time doesn't automatically help a person. Sometimes you may have a spiritual ministry through a warm friendship, where life and spiritual struggles are shared. A college professor was struggling with a deep problem. A close friend came into the office and said, "I have not come to ask or tell you anything. I simply want you to know I am with you." This relationship perhaps helped more than all the "talking" of many people or counselors.

Since separation is the main problem of the young single adult, restoration of relationship is one way you show your ministry.

2. *Relationships—a path to spiritual maturity.* We should never handle people in terms of techniques. The most important approach to a problem is the undergirding relationship. Our attitude is far more important than our method. If we understand people and establish meaningful relationships, we are likely to help them regardless of what techniques we use.

Ministry is communicating the gospel through relationships. Christianity is a relationship. First, man must establish his relationship with God through Jesus Christ. After this relationship is established, then man reaches out in relationship with other men. As man is shut up to himself he stagnates and grows sour. Every man is a potential loner. As we reach out of our shell for a meaningful relationship with another person, we risk ourselves. From the vantage point of God's observation, we could probably see the other reaching out of his shell toward us, also risking himself. If only more lonely persons could see others reaching toward them, more worthy relationships might be formed. A man's worth is measured by his friends or the deep relationships he makes with other people.

People can sit on a jammed commuter train or push their way through a five o'clock rush hour crowd, yet still live in an isolated vacuum. People live in the same apartment building for ten years and yet do not know the other person beyond a name on the mail box.

Mary, a young single adult from Missouri, indicated she wanted to go home. "When I walk down Main Street back home, I nod to people and they smile back, and I feel good. I realize home has second-rate shops, no entertainment, little excitement, and a nine o'clock curfew for teenagers. When I walk down the street in Chicago I feel the excitement of the crowd, the anticipation of looking in the shop windows, and the thrill of being something big, but I'm lonely, and Chicago is an awful place in which to be by yourself.

Mary doesn't need counseling nor does she need to be lectured. The gospel is communicated to her when a Christian reaches out and touches her life. Mary needs to know: She is a sinner but—Christ has paid the price for her sin and—Her heavenly Father accepts her and wants her to grow in—The community of believers which love her.

The average person has a mental image of the church as a building with a steeple, announcement board out front, and a large auditorium. Church is a place where he listens to a sermon, hears soft organ music, and feels the warmth of the sun ray glistening through stained glass windows. If this is what a person thinks, he's wrong. The true church is a community—a body. As the body is made up of many members that depend on each member to do its job, the church is made up of many individuals and depends on each to perform his function. Both the community and body are a maze of interdependent relationships. People need other people as muscles need bones. The church needs people who can help other people.

In a sense, the isolated single adult can appreciate the church more than can his married counterpart. The young married adult has the family, civic organizations, PTA, and a host of other groups all bidding for his time. The young married couple have many opportunities to form friendships. Many of these relationships are forced upon them. As a result, the married couple may look at the church as just another activity in a busy schedule. Church relationships can get lost in the pressures of life. But the single adult can find meaning and significance in life through relationships in the church.

3. *The gospel-content of relationships.* We have talked of man's need—isolation, and the means to solve the problem relationship. Now the content of relationship, the gospel, must be analyzed.

The gospel has two aspects: a proposition and a person. The average church member has only one concept of the gospel: it is a proposition or a statement of faith to believe. Since the gospel has two major aspects, the average church member is limited to half a ministry.

a. *The gospel—a proposition.* The gospel is a concept which we must preach for a person to be born again. Paul outlines explicitly what this gospel is: "I declare unto you the gospel which I preached unto you, which also ye have received, and wherein ye stand . . . that Christ died for our sins according to the scriptures; and that he was buried, and that he rose again the third day according to the scriptures" (I Cor. 15:1-4). The gospel is simply the death, burial, and resurrection of Jesus Christ. This gospel is written in our doctrinal statements or traditionally included in the church's creeds. Without believing in this gospel, a person cannot enter the kingdom of heaven. But the gospel is more.

b. *The gospel—a Person.* The gospel is more than a proposition; it is a Person—Jesus Christ. When the gospel enters our lives, it involves more than giving mental assent to the death, burial, and resurrection of Jesus. The gospel enters our lives when Christ enters our hearts. "But as many as received him (Christ), to them gave he power to become the sons of God" (John 1:12).

The definition of spiritual ministry includes the phrase, "the communication of the gospel." How do we communicate the gospel? We not only sit down and tell the gospel to a person, we live it by being Christians. The gospel in the person of Jesus Christ is in our lives. As we form a meaningful relationship with others, we communicate the gospel of Christ. Therefore, we can have a spiritual ministry by accepting others as a person. We may sit for a time without conversation, but spiritual meaning can be communicated through an understanding or rapport.

The emphasis on relationship of meaning and understanding does not take away from the ministry of talking and listening. Words are the vehicle of expression. When spiritual ministry is effective, there is a deep non-verbal communication of being.

Spiritual ministry "Good Samaritan style" is needed in the twentieth century. Little is recorded of the words spoken by the Good Samaritan, but much is recorded of what he was and what he did. There was an emphatic relationship; the Good Samaritan revealed himself as being kind, selfless, and full of the love of God. A leader who has Christian love shares his life with others.

Since the main problem of people is isolation and loneliness, spiritual ministry through a meaningful relationship can communicate the gospel. If healing of the personality is found in relationships, then spiritual ministry cures the sickness of isolation.

The argument is sometimes heard, "If we don't tell them what to do, how can we know whether they are helped?" The answer is simple: watch for growth by watching for changes in relationships.

CHAPTER EIGHT

UNDERSTANDING PEOPLE'S GOALS

One of the characteristics of living organism is its ability to maintain itself in a state of adjustment or equilibrium. The basic definition of adjustment is to "fit." A person must learn to fit into every situation of life. The term "adjustment" applies to people, and speaks of good or bad adjustment, to fitting a person into the situation in which he finds himself. A farm boy may adjust to a city high school, or to a university campus. A couple just married may adjust or fit into marriage relationship. Adjustment is good or bad as it enables or fails to enable a person to fit into a total situation with a minimum of conflict.

1. *Equilibrium* is the same as satisfaction. The basic drive of a person is to have satisfaction. Just as water seeks its own level, so the human seeks satisfaction in all areas of life (physical, mental, social and psychological). Christians for the most part are ascetic by nature and rebel against the concept that they should seek satisfaction. However, there is an element of truth in the teaching that all humans should have satisfaction. The Scriptures teach that spiritual satisfaction is a valid goal. "thou wilt show me the path of life: in thy presence is fulness of joy; at thy right hand there are pleasures forevermore" (Psalm 16:11) Perhaps the reason most Christians are ascetic is that they feel satisfaction is selfish and they desire to "die to self." The Scriptures do not teach self mortification, but that we have been put to death with Jesus Christ and now we are to act on this historical fact by "reckoning" and "yielding" (Romans 6:11, 13). Our death to self is a once and for all act. Now the Christian is to live for Christ. Living involves a basic state of satisfaction.

God's will is that all Christians live happy satisfying lives. When a person is basically satisfied he is most productive in growth and service. Yet there are some Christians who feel that misery, strife and tension develop inner character. They would desire the believer to suffer unhappiness and go "through the valley of the shadow of death." These people have a martyr complex and don't have a proper understanding of growth. It is not how deep and dark the valley, but what we learn in the valley that causes growth and character. A person who spends all of life in adverse circumstances, with pressures and trials, is not guaranteed a strong character and maturity. The lesson of slums and broken homes teach us that well adjusted, mature people are not the automatic product of such environments. If anything, these environments breed continual misery and unhappiness, generation after generation. Not environment but the lessons from environment produce adjustment and maturity.

BECOMING A LEADER

God would have all Christians live satisfied happy lives, even in the midst of trial. We are to be satisfied with the Lord at all times. A Christian has the right to a happy life and this happy life is expressed in one term—satisfaction. There is only one way to satisfaction and this is through adjustment. A Christian is constantly making adjustment. His life must be adjusted to the will of God. This involves an adjustment in his thinking (mental), his relationship with others (social), his acceptance of his gifts and place in life (psychological), and his walk with God (spiritual).

2. *Drives.* Drives in the human being are an attempt to restore equilibrium. When the body or soul gets out of balance, the person attempts to restore the equilibrium. Such psychologically produced equilibriums are called drives, and these drives might be said to be the basis for activity. When a drive is sustained and there is a prolonged period of unsatisfaction, the result is tension. Adjustment once again brings on satisfaction as tension is alleviated.

3. *Adjustment.* Sometimes, when people are blocked in the activities that may lead to a release of tension, they will substitute another response for the normal response. (For example, the teen who is unsuccessful at school and cannot satisfy his need for social approval by academic success may seek satisfaction by playing up his achievements in other fields of endeavor—by bragging about his love conquests or ability at sports or even an unnatural claim of spirituality.) The youth may withdraw to daydreaming, and by living in a make-believe, imaginary world, he may satisfy his needs by imaginary successes.

4. *Adjustment cycle.* It is characteristic of an organism to remain in a quiescent state when its drives are satisfied. But the ordinary person rarely, if ever, arrives at such a state of perfect balance. Even the well-balanced person who may have a good home, adequate food and clothes, who is happily settled and has a fine group of friends, who is healthy and enjoys life, who may appear to have everything he wants, may need more. He may need more money, more clothes, a more pretentious home, better grades, more popularity and security for life, more love, more power or more than a hundred things to satisfy his needs—the needs that society has created for him.

ADJUSTMENT CYCLE

NEEDS

NEW NEEDS

GOALS

SATISFACTION

DRIVES

ADJUSTMENT

The Christian leader can point out several alternatives to the person in attempting to lead him to a proper adjustment for his situation: (a) why he needs more; (b) satisfaction with present circumstances; (c) proper motivation of desires; (d) how to wait till desires can be provided; (e) ways in which to acquire more; (f) that desires are out of line with necessities.

Maturity is being satisfied with having attained the goal. Yet at the same time maturity is never satisfied because new goals are set up. There are then new drives and a dissatisfaction until the new goal cycle is attained.

The aim of our ministry then is to help people to set up proper attainable goals, establish avenues of gaining these goals, and recognize the state of satisfaction in accomplishment.

This cycle must be repeated over and over, and is known as adjustment. Adjustment must be in every area of life—physical, mental, social, emotional, and spiritual.

CAUSES OF DISSATISFACTION

In the average teenage Sunday School Class, two fifteen-year-old boys may sit together. both come from the same type of background and neighborhood, and both have similar experiences at high school. Yet one boy may live a happy satisfied Christian life, while the other is bound up by fear, tension, and misery. God wants all Christians to live a happy life. What causes one to be well adjusted and the next to be unproductive and miserable? There are many reasons why a Christian may not live a satisfied Christian life. Most of the causes have to do with the person's outlook on life. Money, social standing and popularity do not give basic satisfaction. Some from poor socio-economic backgrounds are well adjusted and satisfied because of a proper outlook on life. Others with material prosperity, popularity and family security are living unhappy and unproductive lives because of an unbalanced adjustment and improper outlook on life.

People do not live happy, prosperous lives—for many reasons. Most of the reasons deal with the inner life and not outer circumstances. If people have properly adjusted their inner drives, abilities and goals, to outer circumstances, demands, and incentives; they can be happy. The following are some inner forces that prevent adjustment.

1. *Goals that are unattainable.* Some face frustration because of unrealistic aims. The twelve-year-old boy saves for a new car and the thirteen-year-old girl falls in love with a college sophomore. When unattainable goals are self-imposed, Christian workers can show the futility of attainment and guide the person to seek that which is within reach, yet still a challenge.

2. *Goals that have no challenge.* Most people do not receive satisfaction in reaching a goal that is too easy. Many times the intelligence of our people is insulted because the goal is not a challenge. Two boys are near

the top of their class academically. Jack has an excellent I.Q. and Bill is an average student. If Jack were to get the highest grade in class without trying, there would be little satisfaction because there was little challenge. If the average student, Bill, got the top honors it would mean more to him. The greater the challenge the greater the satisfaction. "To do the easier when the harder is possible constitutes the greatest tragedy in life."

3. *Goals that are too long-range.* Everyone should have a long-range goal in life. This involves what they will be, what kind of life they will live, what type of person they will marry, etc. However, to have a long-range goal with no step-by-step plan is frustrating. The person is fooling himself when he has a long-range goal to be an architect, yet makes no plans for preparation in high school courses. This person is always desiring and never arriving. He can't have satisfaction and adjustment.

People should have vision—and not illusion. The mature, well adjusted person can think in terms of a goal and the means to that goal.

4. *Goals that are only short-range.* "Tomorrow" or next time is the password to immaturity. Many can think only in terms of short-range goals. These people are usually happy and satisfied, yet don't have a blueprint for their lives. Short-term goals are usually tangents. Those who choose day-to-day goals may find themselves steering away from a productive course.

Life is like a golf game. As long as we go straight off the tee, down the fairway to the green, everything is fine. When a person gets lost in the woods, he loses all sense of direction. A wise leader will always direct the person to an ultimate pattern of life in keeping with the will of God.

5. *Goals set by someone else.* Many find themselves walking down a path in life that brings no happiness. This path may be the choice of mother or homeroom teacher. Some boys are forced to go to college because father never had the chance. Girls find themselves pushed into early sophistication by domineering mothers. Most find happiness when they live their own lives. Of course freedom is within the limits of God's standards.

When the leaders deal with people who have had their goals set by someone else, the problem is compounded. Both persons need help. If the problem is compounded by a parent, the leader must respect parental authority, yet lead the youth to self-determined goals in life.

6. *Goals too high for inner ability.* All too often, someone will choose a goal that is possible but not probable. A boy with an extremely low I.Q. may choose to go to college. A girl who does not have grace or natural beauty will choose a modeling career. How to deal with these people constitutes a problem. Is it wrong to encourage them to do what they cannot do? To dissuade them may be cutting the vine from the branch. There are several reasons why goals are too high for inner ability: (a) some won't have the background; (b) some lack social training; (c) some lack ability;

(d) some lack experience; (e) lack of money also hinders arriving at a goal.

Leaders will need to understand the nature of people, then help them form worthy goals in life. When people choose goals below or beyond their capacity they shortchange themselves. Attainment of a worthy goal can bring satisfaction and lead to growth and maturity.

GOALS OF ADJUSTMENT

The Bible teaches adjustment or satisfaction. This is seen through several scriptural qualities. These qualities are available for all believers. Since these qualities are expanded in many other sources, the following explanation is not comprehensive, but shows the relationship between the scriptural qualities of life and adjustment. Spiritual adjustment is being rightly related to the will of God and the Word of God.

1. *Goal of adjustment—peace.* Peace in the Bible is seen in at least two ways:

(a) *Peace with God*—the work of Christ on the cross, into which the believer enters at conversion. This truth is seen in Ephensians 2:14-17; Romans 5:1. The person must enter into the "peace of God" relationship.

(b) *Peace of God*—The inward tranquility or satisfaction of the believer who commits his anxieties to God. The person who would experience *peace of God* must first experience *peace with God.* At this point the leader should realize he cannot lead a person to true peace of soul until the question of salvation is settled.

The peace of God is promised to the believer if he deals with anxieties. "Be careful for nothing; but in everything by prayer and supplication with thanksgiving let your requests be made known unto God. And the peace of God . . . shall keep your hearts and minds through Christ Jesus" (Phil. 4:6, 7). Note the realm of peace is "through Christ Jesus." The means of peace is through the release of prayer, and the results of peace come after anxieties are satisfied. Therefore, the peace of God and adjustment are the same thing.

Note that the peace of God has no equal in worldly adjustment. Christ promised peace that the world could not give. "Peace I leave with you, my peace I give unto you: not as the world giveth" (John 14:27). Beware of trying to bring satisfaction into a person's life apart from spiritual adjustment. Spiritual adjustment is being rightly related to the will of God and the Word of God. If a person is divorced from the ministry of the Lord and the Word of God, there can be no peace. "These things I have spoken unto you, that in time ye might have peace. In the world ye shall have tribulation" (John 16:33). Here Christ indicates the person will have inner anxieties, frustrations and misery apart from the Word of God. I have counseled people on several occasions apart from spiritual truth and dynamics. I have felt inclined to deal with mental doubts only in philosophical reactions. On these occasions I failed by not throwing the light of the Word of God on the problem. Christ has promised that peace comes through him. There-fore, leaders should realize that inner satisfaction and peace come only as God's perspective enlightens the problems.

2. *Goal of adjustment—satisfaction.* A Christian is commanded to find satisfaction in his Master. "Delight thyself also in the LORD; and he shall give thee the desires of thine heart" (Psalm 37:4). The drive to have satis-faction or delight must be filled. This drive for satisfaction was placed in a person's psychological and biological make-up. Don't blame the person for these urges; they are following the compelling urges of the inner man. Blame should be directed for the way he satisfies this urge, not for the fact of these urges.

When a person is rightly adjusted to the will of God, the result is satis-faction. "Not doing thine own ways, nor finding thine own pleasure, nor speaking thine own words: then shalt thou delight thyself in the LORD" (Isaiah 58:13, 14).

3. *Goal of adjustment—joy.* The Christian should live a life of joy, happiness and satisfaction. Joy comes only as a result of the Christian's being in right adjustment to God—the source of joy. "The joy of the LORD is your strength" (Nehemiah 8:10). Joy is the positive reaction of fulfilled desires and drives. "Thou wilt show me the path of life: in thy presence is fulness of joy; at thy right hand there are pleasures for ever-more" (Psalm 16:11). The Christian is commanded to have joy and express it to others. "Rejoice in the Lord alway: and again I say, Rejoice" (Phil. 4:4).

The youth leader must understand the source and secret of joy. People demand and need happiness. This does not mean we are to give in to their selfish demands or treat them as children. True obedience to God's Word brings joy. Perhaps a leader can help people find joy and satisfaction in obeying the commands of God's Word.

4. *Goal of adjustment—maturity.* The aim of adjustment and satisfac-tion is maturity. Adjustment and satisfaction are the immediate aims of ministry. The long-range goal is maturity. The next chapter deals with maturity.

CHAPTER NINE

UNDERSTANDING MATURITY

Because of fuzzy thinking, people are not always sure of the word "mature". When is a boy mature? A growing boy reaches optimum physical growth at twenty-two years of age. A growing girl reaches optimum physical development at seventeen years of age. Can we say the seventeen-year old couple that go steady is half and half? She is mature but the boy is not? How much more mature does she become at age twenty-two?

DEFINITION OF MATURITY

When is a mature person mature? Can a thirteen-year old boy be mature? Does one become mature at twenty-one? How old do you have to be to become mature?

There are two definitions of maturity. First, maturity is seen as a sliding scale; while second, maturity is viewed as a final destination.

1. *Maturity—sliding scale concept.* In a class a teacher will sometimes grade on the curve if the whole class scores low; some will automatically pass and some will automatically fail. The curve is relative. Applying this to the grading of maturity, maturity is a relative thing. A twelve-year old boy is considered mature when he displays all the qualities of twelve-year old-ness. When a boy displays the physical looks of a twelve-year-old boy, the social attitudes and actions, and the satisfactory psychological adjustment for a twelve-year old boy, we say he is mature for age twelve.

Those twelve-year old boys who display a level of life equal to age ten are said to be immature. We say those boys who are developed beyond their age are advanced beyond maturity.

Those who hold to a sliding scale concept of maturity feel that a boy can be mature all his life. As he maintains the expected rate of development, he remains mature. A boy can be a mature five-year-old, a mature ten-year-old, and ultimately a mature twenty-year-old.

Those who think maturity is relative feel that an adult can be forty and be immature. A forty-year old woman who does not display forty-year old characteristics is immature. Hence, maturity is not only relative, but it is not permanent. A person must continue to grow to continue to be mature. The forty-year-old woman may be immature at forty, but may have been a mature twenty-year-old. She stopped developing with advancing age and stopped maturing. In one sense, we are always approaching maturity but never mature; always growing but never fully develop.

2. *Maturity—adulthood (final destination).* The second concept states that maturity is synonymous with adulthood. When a child is half grown,

he is half mature. When a teenager is almost grown, he is almost mature. Maturity is viewed as an unchanging goal toward which all growth is aimed. The goal of physical, mental, social, emotional, and spiritual growth is maturity. Once we reach that elusive age we become mature and hold it for the rest of our lives.

Those who feel that maturity is the unchanging goal of development say most people reach this aim in the late teens or early twenties. Some never reach maturity and go through life as immature adults.

3. *Maturity in the Scriptures.* The Bible seems to teach maturity as an unchanging goal. Although the word "maturity" does not occur in the Word of God, the teaching is surely there. The word "perfection" usually carries the meaning of maturity. In the verse "For the perfecting of the saints" (Eph. 4:12), the word used comes from the root word "perfective" meaning "to mend the nets". When a fisherman mends the nets they are made complete or whole. Maturity is seen as the man who is complete or whole in every area of life.

Ephesians 4:11-16 is the key passage on the teaching of maturity. In verse 14 we are told not to be like children, because children are unstable: **"That we henceforth be no more children, tossed to and fro, and carried** about with every wind of doctrine." A mark of maturity is stability, and children who are not mature are unstable. The passage applies to doctrinal **maturity but can be related to every area of life. Be mature, be stable, like** full-grown adults.

The passage teaches that maturity is equal to the "perfect man, unto the measure of the stature of the fulness of Christ" (Eph. 4:13). Maturity is the goal of spiritual development that comes at the end of the growth process. We do not find the Scriptures calling a babe in Christ mature. We are to "grow up into him in all things, which is the head" (Eph. 4:15). The standard of physical maturity is the average man. The standard of spiritual maturity is likeness to Christ.

4. *Maturity—quality not quantity.* Maturity is a measure of quality. It is not how much one does that determines maturity; it is what one does with the opportunities at hand that determines maturity. Maturity is not how old one looks but is measured by one's outlook. We are as mature as the way we see life. Maturity is not measured by observation of our physical features. Maturity is measured by our view on life and other people.

It is difficult to measure maturity, for one may be mature mentally but very immature in his social adjustment. Physically, a boy may be nineteen but spiritually the same boy is only ten years old. Is he mature?

MEASURES OF MATURITY

Some of the following measures may help us determine maturity. These criteria should be applied to all areas of development—physical, mental, social, emotional, sexual, and spiritual.

1. *Maturity thinks by a blueprint.* The person who has the ability to base his judgment on the big picture—the long haul—is the mature individual. You should realize that you are guiding people to mature decisions—to the extent that people are guided by the long-term purposes rather than the immediate desires.

Children are immature. This is seen in their play. Only that which brings immediate satisfaction is enjoyed. The older one becomes, the more he is able to control emotions because of the consequences. As a person learns to control the emotion and discipline himself, he can live by an over-all plan of life. Marriage is a long-term agreement into which only mature people should enter. Maturity is seen by a person's habit of saving money or accumulating college credits, realizing he is making a record in life. Drink, sexual promiscuity and dope have no long-range purpose. The mature person is the one who is able to pass up the fun-for-the-minute and select a course of action that will pay off later. One of the characteristics of babyhood is "I want it now." The mature person can wait.

2. *Maturity finds satisfaction in things as they are.* The mature person is able to accept things and people the way they are rather than pretend they are the way he wants them to be. Picture a child playing. Life is all harmony and happiness. Everything comes out fine in the end. This is the usual climax of a TV program. However, life is not this way. There are many disappointments and unhappy periods of life. The person who can accept unhappiness along with happiness has begun to mature in life. Maturity is the capacity to face unpleasantness, frustration, discomfort, and defeat without complaint or collapse. Many persons run away from life. Some will retrogress to former childhood activity. High schoolers will date junior high girls. Some will escape to sleep because in slumber they lose their problems in the unconscious. The mature person knows he cannot have everything his own way. He is able to wait on circumstances, on other people, and on time.

Many people resort to daydreaming. They find wonderful satisfaction in the childhood world of make-believe. However, they are not mature by retreating from life as it is.

3. *Maturity makes a decision and sticks to it.* The mature person is the one who is able to accept his own role in life as a decision maker. The adult who constantly is changing jobs, changing friends, changing mates, and changing his life is an immature adult. He cannot stick to anything because he is not mature. The mature person is one who can make a decision and live with the consequences. When things go well, he does not have a sense of bravado or sense of guilt. The mature person learns from his mistakes rather than finding excuses for them. The immature person will rationalize his mistake. He will place the blame on someone else or refuse to admit that there was any mistake at all. Maturity will rectify rather than justify.

Maturity is the ability to live responsibly. This involves dependability.

BECOMING A LEADER

To be mature is to be dependable. Some people never seem to come through in a pinch. The person who breaks his promise, who is always late or never shows up at all, who cannot be depended on, is immature. For the most part, such people are confused, disorganized, and purposeless in life. Their lives are empty. Immaturity can be filed under the topic "unfinished business." Immature people spend their lives exploring endless possibilities. They look up job opportunities and then do nothing about them. Action requires courage; there is no maturity without courage.

4. *Maturity has the ability to love.* Many have difficulty expressing love to other people. The immature person needs constant reassurance of being loved. The immature person demands feeling, romance or sentiment. But love becomes only a feeling, it is nothing more than self-satisfaction. To the immature, love is primarily receiving, not giving. The Bible has said it is more blessed to give than to receive. Love is giving of your self to another. Many people are unable to give; often they think only in terms of what they are going to receive.

Love is an action expressing our responsibility for the needs of others. The immature person who is preoccupied with his own need is lonely. The test enemy that keeps many from growing is the inability to express love. Christ expressed the apex of love when he said, "Greater love hath no man than this, that a man lay down his life for his friends" (John 15:13). The love and maturity is giving of yourself for another. Those who do not have the ability to give themselves do not have the ability to love.

5. *Maturity accepts the authority of others.* The person who is mature has the ability to live up to his responsibilities. This means being dependable. When a person accepts responsibility or the authority of another, he must do so without rebellion. Many teenagers are defiant of authority. Rebellion to authority is a childhood trait.

A teenager is a strange mixture of child and adult. At one time a child is under the direction of an adult, and in the process of growing up he becomes equal with adults. As he grows older he becomes more defiant. Picture the teenager who is rebellious to his parents, teachers or employer. The teenager who rebels against getting to school on time, speed limits or waiting in line at the store is immature. Yet there is some rebellious adolescence in most people.

6. *Maturity has a proper self-understanding.* Socrates said, "Know thyself." The mature person is one who is able to understand himself, defend himself, and direct himself. A proper evaluation of one's abilities and one's attitudes leads to satisfaction and proper growth. Everyone in life has impulses. The method of dealing with our impulses determines our maturity. For the most part immature people do not deal with their impulses correctly. They find scapegoats and blame others. Some attack other people verbally and sometimes physically. They have a false and spurious sense of security.

The aims of ministry are conversion and growth. These immediate aims are sometimes difficult to verbalize or implement in a life. But ultimate goals should nevertheless remain the constant guidepost, pointing leaders to a specific aim. Between the immediate ministry and the ultimate goal are years of work. The leader may get lost from one meeting to the next unless there are clear ultimate goals.

THE GOAL OF MATURITY

The following objectives are listed to give the church counselor guidance to ultimate goals. Many have attempted to list the objectives of a church program for youth. To be complete, such a list would be as lengthy as the New Testament. This list grew out of a Christian Education Workshop on youth work in Grant Memorial Baptist Church, Winnipeg, Manitoba. The author makes no claim for completeness of thought.

CHRISTIAN CONVERSION

Our aim is to lead each unsaved young person to a genuine experience of the forgiving and saving grace of God through Jesus Christ. This means helping each one:

1. To become aware of the nature and prevalence of sin and to recognize God's judgment upon it;

2. To realize his own sin and his consequent need of the salvation which God has provided in Christ;

3. To turn from sin and commit himself to Jesus Christ, the Son of God, who gives complete salvation to all who trust him;

4. To gain, after conversion, a growing sense of assurance as to the reality of that experience and its implications in terms of the lordship of Jesus.

CHRISTIAN KNOWLEDGE AND CONVICTION

Our aim is to help each young person to grow toward mature Christian knowledge, understanding, and conviction. This means helping each one:

1. With respect to the Bible—

(a) to recognize the Bible as the only revelation from God and to accept its authority as supreme in matters of faith and conduct;

(b) to gain fuller understanding of the origins of the Bible, the history of its preservation, and the significance of many translations and versions;

(c) to achieve an increasing knowledge of Bible content and a growing understanding of the customs, geography, and history out of which the Bible came;

(d) to acquire a growing comprehension of how Bible truths apply to personal daily living, to family life, and how to commit choice passages to memory.

2. With respect to the great realities of the Christian faith—

BECOMING A LEADER

(a) to grow in understanding of the nature, attributes, and will of God;

(b) to grow in understanding of the nature of man, of sin and salvation, and of the varied elements of Christian experience;

(c) to grow in understanding of the Christian concepts of personal holiness and social responsibility;

(d) to develop a growing conviction about truth and the finality of the Christian faith.

3. With respect to the Christian movement—

(a) to know something of the general outline of Christian history;

(b) to learn some of the outstanding facts about other Christian groups and our common heritage with them;

(c) to grow in understanding of present-day trends and issues in the Christian movement and to develop ability to evaluate their significance of life, the church and the cause of Christ throughout the world.

CHRISTIAN LIVING

Our aim is to guide each young person in developing habits and skills which promote spiritual growth and in applying Christian standards of conduct in every area of life. This means helping each one:

1. To live daily in vital fellowship with Jesus Christ, seeking always to bring the whole life under the direction of the Holy Spirit.

2. To engage regularly in serious Bible study and to use the Bible as a guide for life.

3. To understand the value of prayer and to practice prayer in daily experience.

4. To pattern all of his personal conduct in accordance with the teachings, spirit, and example of Jesus Christ.

5. To do all possible to make his home life Christian.

6. To refuse to enter into relationships and participate in activities which compromise or violate New Testament principles.

7. To seek to apply Christian principles and standards of conduct to all social relationships.

CHRISTIAN ATTITUDES AND APPRECIATION

Our aim is to assist each young person in developing such Christian attitudes and appreciations that he will have a Christian approach to all of life. This means helping each one;

1. Regarding God—

(a) to **reverence** God, respect his commandments, and seek to know and to do his will as the supreme good;

(b) to love and trust the Heavenly Father, Jesus Christ as Lord and Saviour, and the Holy Spirit as ever-present counselor and source of power;

(c) to develop a sense of gratitude to God for all his goodness.

2. Regarding the meaning of existence—

(a) to regard all existence as the expression of God's creative power, wisdom, and goodness;

(b) to see himself in relation to all existence in such a way as to feel secure in the purpose and sovereignty of God;

(c) to regard life as a trust from God to be used for his glory and the good of others;

(d) to believe with confidence that the Bible and the Holy Spirit are God's guides in making the best use of his life;

(e) to believe that the main purposes of God for mankind are redemption and development in holiness.

3. Regarding self—

(a) to realize that as a person created in the image of God, he is of infinite worth and has marvelous possibilities;

(b) to realize that he stands in continuing need of forgiveness and strength from God;

(c) to recognize that he possesses spiritual needs and capacities which only God can supply;

(d) to acknowledge that his body is a divine trust to be cared for, to be protected from abuse, to be disciplined in habit, and to be used in honest labor, unselfish service, and healthful recreation;

(e) to dedicate all of his God-given abilities to the pursuit and achievement of worthy aims and to test their worthiness by the teachings of Jesus;

(f) to have as his personal ideal the attainment of a mature, well-balanced Christian personality.

4. Regarding others—

(a) to cultivate an attitude of Christian love, the willingness to practice forgiveness, and the determination to apply Christian principles in all his relationships;

(b) to accept responsibility for the influence of his life upon all people whom his life touches;

(c) to develop wholesome attitudes toward other young people of the opposite sex;

(d) to cultivate a sense of belonging to the human race as a whole;

(e) to develop an attitude of Christian concern for the welfare of people of all cultures, social levels, and races;

(f) to feel a responsibility to pass on to future generations the good in his social heritage enriched by his own contribution to it.

5. Regarding the Bible and divine institutions—

(a) to develop a growing love for the Bible and an appreciation of the relevance of Bible teaching to daily life;

(b) to respect the divine nature and purpose of the church and to

BECOMING A LEADER

give it a place of sacred pre-eminence over all institutions ot human origin;

(c) to respect Baptism and the Lord's Supper and to seek through their observance to honor Christ;

(d) to regard Sunday as the Lord's Day to be used to the honor of the risen Christ;

(e) to accept the standards set by Christ and the New Testament for marriage and family life;

(f) to respect the institution of civil government and accept the responsibilities of good citizenship.

6. Regarding the present world—

(a) to feel that the world as God made it is good and that all the resources of nature and the necessity to work are gifts of God designed for the enrichment of life;

(b) to recognize that evil is a dominant force in the world order and that the Christian, while he must live in this world, is not to share its spirit nor indulge in its sins but is to resist evil and be a positive force for morality and justice;

(c) to develop a deepening consciousness of responsibility for the social order of which he is a part and a courageous purpose to work for its improvement.

CHRISTIAN WORSHIP

Our aim is to help each young person make Christian worship a vital and constant part of his expanding experience. This means helping each one:

1. To develop a deepening understanding of the meaning and values of worship;

2. To develop a growing appreciation of all the elements that make for meaningful worship, both private and corporate;

3. To develop and maintain the practice of daily individual worship, including the devotional reading of the Bible, meditation, and prayer;

4. To develop the habit of regular attendance of the public services of his church and the ability to participate in these services with understanding and appreciation;

5. To encourage and to participate in experiences of family worship.

CHRISTIAN SERVICE

Our aim is to lead each young person to make maximum contribution to the cause of Christ in keeping with his spiritual gifts. This means helping each one:

1. To seek and use opportunities to invest his talents and skills in Christian service;

2. To witness consistently to truth and power of the Christian faith and seek to win others to Jesus Christ;

3. To work faithfully for the building up of his church and to serve sacrificially in and through his church;

4. To give of his money, from worthy motives and according to biblical teaching, for the support of his church and its work;

5. To show compassion for persons in need and do deeds of helpfulness in his daily life;

6. To find God's will for his life, to prepare adequately for the vocation to which he is called, and to enter that vocation with a sense of dedication to Christian Service.

7. To serve effectively as a member of a team and to serve without desire for self-glory;

8. To dedicate his total personality and resources to world missions as the means of carrying forward the redemptive undertaking of Jesus Christ;

9. To co-operate with others in the improvement of social conditions, the creation of a more Christian society, and the realization of God's purpose for mankind.

CONCLUSION

Blessed are the unsatisfied when they have a goal. Many are unsatisfied and their lives are filled with frustration. Christianity does not have a goal for people—it is a goal. Lives should be productive for Christ, satisfying to the person, profitable to the church and counting for eternity. They could be, if leaders understood biblical goals and then translated these goals into challenges for others. The church could save countless wasted lives if people had a scriptural challenging goal.

Blessed are the unsatisfied when they have a goal.

CHAPTER TEN

UNDERSTANDING THE CALL TO FULL-TIME SERVICE

Often Christian young people deal with the question, "Am I called to full-time Christian service?" Sometimes this is reduced to the questions, "Have you got the call?" The call or calling of God is a term that indicates a person has been chosen by God and separated from a secular vocation to serve the Lord in a full-time vocational manner so that his total pursuit of life is occupied with the aims of the New Testament, for which he receives a salary, the church becoming obligated for his financial responsibility. Usually, the call of God involves a lifetime separation to the ministry. However, not all people who are called are financially supported by the church. Many young people studying for the ministry are supported by their family or they work to put themselves through school. Even after entering the ministry, some will work in secular employment (tent making) while pioneering a work for God.

The ministry is more than an occupation or a job, it is a call from God. The salary is lower than most other positions of equal responsibility. The demands are great, the hours are long, the burdens are almost unbearable. Ministers are gossiped about and lied about. They are criticized to their faces, and carnal church members connive behind their backs. The pastorate is one of the most demanding positions and no one man could remain as pastor without the inner assurance that the Almighty God has called him to that office.

What makes a minister give up sleep to prepare sermons and pray for power on his message? The call of God. What motivates a minister to spend all day knocking on doors instead of getting a better-paying job when he knows his family doesn't have as nice things as the neighbors or he doesn't have the freedom to be with his family as much as some others? What possesses a man's heart to lay brick on a church, to paint old pews, to run a mimeograph, to get on the radio and preach the gospel? The call of God.

A man at the assembly line hears something none others perceive—it is God's call. He begins to march to a different drumbeat: it is God's command to go and build a church, even when his friends think he is crazy. A man attempts to do what seems impossible. He speaks in public when his grammar is shoddy; he knocks on doors, knowing he cannot sell. He attempts to teach the Bible when he has little formal education. He tries to build huge auditoriums, not knowing construction or architecture. He manages a large corporation, though ignorant of financing or advertising. Why does a man dream the unthinkable and attempt the impossible? He feels God has called him and all he can do is obey. This minister knows that with God's calling is God's enablement and that if God has called him, he can serve the Lord.

The ministry is not something a man chooses. A young man does not look through the want ads and, not finding a position, turn to the pastorate. The New Testament church begins with a God-called man who is willing to make any sacrifice, to pay any price, to forsake all and build a church in the name and after the pattern of Jesus Christ who said, "I will build my church" (Matt. 16:18).

THE BIBLICAL VIEW OF CALL

Even though the term *call* or *calling* has a technical use in today's church, it is used in three ways in Scripture. First, the call to salvation, second the call to sanctification, and third, the call to full-time Christian service.

1. *The Call to Salvation.* In Scripture the word *call* is designated as the invitation of Jesus Christ for a person to become saved. Jesus said, "Come unto me all ye that labour and are heavy laden, and I will give you rest" (Matt. 11:28) In essence, He was calling people to salvation. Later Paul designates this call, "Among whom are ye also the called of Jesus Christ" (Rom. 1:6). He also tells us that, "All things work together for good to them that love God, to them who are the called according to His purpose" (Rom. 8:28). We know this refers to salvation because everyone who is called is ultimately justified and glorified (vs. 30). Paul reminds the Thessalonians that he was praying for them that, "Our God would count you worthy of this calling". (II Thess. 1:11).

Jesus was pictured as a shepherd who leaves the ninety-nine safely in the fold and goes out into the wilderness, calling His one lost sheep. The call of God is reflected in the words of the hymn: "Softly and tenderly, Jesus is calling . . . calling today". Every time a minister ends his sermon and begins the invitation, he is calling men to repentance; he is calling men to Jesus Christ.

The call to salvation has scriptural precedent. Jesus called Zacchaeus down from a tree. Jesus told the woman at the well, "Go, call thy husband"—symbolic of bringing him to salvation. Many churches entitle their visitation program "Calling". Even though they mean ringing doorbells, it is symbolic of the call that every sinner should be called to salvation.

Paul prayed for the Ephesians, "The eyes of your understanding being enlightened; that ye may know what is the hope of his calling" (Eph. 1:18). They were called in hope, then they became partakers of the heavenly calling of God (Heb. 3:1). This calling extends to all people. Paul specifies that everyone is called to salvation, "For ye see your calling, brethren, how that not many wise men after the flesh, not many mighty, not many noble, are called" (I Cor. 1:26). But ye are a chosen generation, a royal priesthood, an holy nation, a peculiar people; that ye should show forth the praises of him who hath called you out of darkness into his marvelous light" (I Peter 2:9).

2. *The Call to Sanctification.* God not only calls man to salvation, but he also calls them to grow to completion or maturity in Jesus Christ. This is a call to sanctification. Paul reminds the Corinthians that, "God is faithful, by whom ye were called into the fellowship of His Son Jesus Christ our Lord" (I Cor. 1:9). He had already indicated that the Corinthians knew Christ as Saviour, but to this carnal church, he was inviting them to grow deeper in fellowship with Jesus Christ.

Paul explains further the call to sanctification when writing to the Philippians, "That I may know Him, and the power of His resurrection, and the fellowship of His sufferings, being made conformable unto his death" (Phil. 3:10). Paul had already known Jesus Christ in salvation, now he wanted a daily walk with Jesus Christ so that the life of the resurrection flowed through him. He even realized that suffering was a part of knowing Jesus Christ in an intimate manner. He explains that Christ is the object of fellowship and the resurrection is the power of fellowship. Paul's appeal for them goes deeper with God and climaxes, "I press toward the mark for the prize of the high calling of God in Christ Jesus" (Phil. 3:14). The high call for every Christian is to be as sanctified as possible in fellowship with Jesus Christ.

3. *The Call to Full-time Christian Service.* The greatest honour that can come to any person is to be set aside by the Holy Spirit to serve Jesus Christ with all of his life. These are identified as those who are in the professional ministry. Today they are pastors, assistant pastors, evangelists, missionaries, Bible teachers in colleges, and others who serve in full-time ministry; by which they are supported financially full-time. In the Old Testament, the high priests were full-time Christian servants. "No man taketh this honour unto himself, but he that is called of God, as was Aaron" (Heb. 5:4). This verse gives us insight into full-time Christian service. In the Old Testament a priest had to be born into the tribe of Levi, but not every Levite became a priest. Only those who were called of God were set aside for actual service in the temple.

Barnabas and Paul were called of God to full-time Christian service. Remember even at Paul's conversion it was indicated that he would be a unique servant and messenger to the Gentiles (Acts 9:15-16). However, after 14 years of learning and apprenticeship, by serving Jesus Christ in the church at Damascus, Tarsus, and Antioch; Paul was ready to be separated into full-time Christian service. We read the account, "As they ministered to the Lord, and fasted, the Holy Ghost said, "Separate me Barnabas and Saul for the work whereunto I have called them" (Acts 13:2). Note that these two men who were called into full-time Christian service were actively involved in serving Jesus Christ. The call did not come to two unconcerned high school boys who were sitting on the last pew in the church. These were active church leaders who were called into full-time Christian service.

A second part of the call is that they were to be separated, indicating they were no longer considered laymen. A third part of the call to full-time service was accompanied with self-examination and searching the mind of the Lord. Barnabas and Saul were fasting and praying to the Lord when they were called. Notice the verse begins, "as". They were in the process of serving the Lord when they were called. A last part of the call is that it came from the Holy Spirit. No man can issue the call to himself. He can desire the office of a bishop (I Tim. 3:7), but the call of God comes from the Holy Spirit.

When Jesus Christ walked along the shore of Galilee, He called Peter and Andrew to follow Him. This illustrates the call of God. They had to give up their nets (occupation) and follow Jesus Christ full-time. Even in this illustration we see the place of a Christian college or a seminary. The call to full-time Christian service is also the call to prepare. They were called to follow Jesus Christ, but for three years they were sitting at His feet, learning how to be disciples.

When Paul wrote to the Romans, he identified himself as "Paul, a servant of Jesus Christ, called to be an apostle" (Rom. 1:1). In the same manner, every minister of Jesus Christ can identify himself as one who is called to serve Jesus Christ.

Deeply convicted during a Sunday evening church service, Tom Berry went home unsaved. Alone with his Bible at home later, on his knees he prayed, "Lord, if You will save me, You can have all of me". He knew if he were to be saved, Christ would have to do the saving. Later in Canton, Texas, while milking a cow, he felt in his heart that God was calling him to preach. He went in the house and announced his decision to his mother, who was shocked; young Tom had been a jokester in school. But God sometimes uses other men to help confirm a call to the ministry. Tom Berry spent a Saturday night at the Texas State Fair in Dallas carousing around. When he got home, he was burdened and he felt God telling him, "I've called you to preach and here you are messing around with sin." About 2:30 a.m. he made a complete surrender. As he reached the parking lot of the church, his pastor said, "Tom, what are you going to do with your life?" Three weeks later he was in college preparing for the ministry.

Saved as a teenager, John Powell, pastor of Reimer Road Baptist Church, Wadsworth, Ohio, was out of the will of God for a number of years. After his rededication as a young husband and father, he began to teach in the Sunday School. A year later, he felt God was calling him into the ministry. One Sunday when a missionary speaker did not show up, his pastor spoke on "Being a Missionary at Home". At the invitation, Powell wanted to go forward but was afraid. Finally, he went forward in surrender to the ministry, and found that God had been speaking to his wife in another section of the church—she too had come forward. Powell told the pastor, "I think God is calling me into the ministry." The pastor boldly announced, "John has surrendered for the ministry".

Bruce Cummons, of the Massillon Baptist Temple, was a diligent young man, serving God in the Akron Baptist Temple after his return from military service. One evening he was so burdened that he went walking by Lake Erie, stretching himself out on the grass to pray. The burden would not leave. Finally, he said in desperation, "Lord, I'll do anything . . . I'll preach the gospel if you want me to." Immediately the burden lifted, and Bruce knew that God had called him to preach the gospel. Until that time he was not aware that God was speaking to him about the ministry. Young Samuel in the tabernacle heard the audible voice of God in the night. God had to call three times before Eli recognized it was God and told the young boy to say, "Speak . . . for thy servant heareth" (I Sam. 3:10). It was not until Samuel responded correctly that he knew God was calling him.

Many times God calls through another person. As the elderly prophet Elijah, stood before God in Mt. Sinai, God called him to go and anoint his successor, Elisha. We have the record in I Kings 19:19-21 of the old man throwing his mantle across young Elisha's shoulders as he plowed. God uses his servants to extend a call to young men. Ed Nelson, pastor of the South Sheridan Baptist Church, had led singing for a revival by Dr. Bob Jones, Jr. It was during the Second World War years and most of the young men were in service. He confessed he was not a good song leader but did the best he could; there was no one else available. An elderly lady came to the platform and looked up at young Ed as he bent over to speak to her. "Ed, I believe God is calling you to the ministry." He slapped his knee and exclaimed, "that's the funniest thing I have ever heard!" Several in the auditorium heard his loud response but the lady got him to promise to pray about it. Eight days later, he was plowing sugar beets before the sun came up on a Monday morning; the burden of God was driving him to desperation. Ed Nelson got off the tractor and knelt in the wet sod, surrendering for the ministry. God had used a saintly grandmother to reach his heart.

Led to Jesus Christ in the home of a soul winner at Highland Park Baptist Church, Chattanooga, Bob Kelley made his public profession in a Lester Roloff revival meeting. His pastor, Dr. Lee Roberson, said as Kelley prepared for baptism, "I believe that boy will preach some day." Bob Kelley never escaped Dr. Roberson's comment. Three years later in a revival meeting he felt the call to preach the gospel. Kelley gave up a grant-in-aid athletic scholarship and transferred to Tennessee Temple Schools to prepare for the ministry.

A hundred and thirty-two young men have gone into full-time Christian service from Trinity Baptist Church, Jacksonville, Florida as of 1975. The powerful preaching of Bob Gray won many of these young boys, and they were eventually called to full-time service. Just as Gray's preaching produced young preacher boys, so Paul reminds Timothy, "Neglect not the gift that is in thee, which was given thee by prophecy" (I Tim. 4:14), indicating that the gift to serve God came as Paul used his gift of prophecy, which was preaching the gospel.

When Paul preached, young men were called to preach the gospel. With the calling comes the enablement (spiritual gifts) to serve God. If a church is effectively preaching the gospel and teaching the Word of God, then young men will be called into full-time Christian service. If a church doesn't have young people going into the Lord's service, then something is wrong with its ministry. If a church has not had a young man surrender to preach in the past ten years, then perhaps God has removed the candlestick from the church.

"The call of God was permission to me" testified Don Young, Bible Baptist Church, Paducah, Kentucky. Young had been in college and had thought of becoming a pastor, yet was not rebellious to the Lord. He testified, "When God said "preach", I did not take it as a command, but as His willingness to allow me to serve Him . . . it was His permission". Young described the great relief and joy that came to his heart with the call of God. He replied, "I will preach." I just wanted to preach anywhere, anytime that God gave me a great desire to preach His Word."

A DEFINITION OF CALL TO FULL-TIME SERVICE

When I attend an ordination service I always ask the candidate the following question, "What is the call of God and how do you know that you have it?" I feel that if a candidate cannot identify the call of God and convince the council that he has been called to full-time Christian service, then we should not ordain him no matter how much theological knowledge he has. Ordination is a serious matter, and no one should have "hands laid on him" if there is not absolute assurance that he has been called into full-time Christian service.

Once a young man answered the question by indicating the command in Scripture was the call of God. He noted since Jesus had commanded to go and preach the gospel to everyone, he should do so. This answer was not enough. Surely the call of God is based on the command of Scripture. But, the command of God is given to everyone. Every Christian should preach the gospel to all people. That is the basis for the call. But the call to full-time Christian service is more than the command of Scripture. It is a unique experience that only those who have been set aside by Jesus Christ have received. The command of Scripture is to everyone. The call of God is more particular. It is only to the recipients.

Then the candidate gave a second basis for the call of God. He said the call of God was the need of people to hear the gospel. He went on to indicate that there were thousands of needy people in the city who needed to get saved. Once again the candidate had to be corrected. The need is an obligation upon every Christian, but the need alone is not the call. Every Christian meets needy people every day of his life, but this does not constitute a call to full-time Christian service. The call is based upon the need of **people to hear the gospel, but the call of God to full-time Christian service** is a unique experience that goes beyond the obligation of every Christian.

Therefore the call to full-time Christian service can be described in three ways: first desire, second burden, and third by fruit.

1. *The call of God begins with a burden.* Several of the Old Testament prophets indicated that their message was the burden of the Lord (Mal. 1:1; Hab. 1:1). A burden is an obligation or a compulsion. A young man who is called into full-time Christian service has a burden or a compulsion to serve Jesus Christ. The need of lost people adds to the burden he gets from Scripture, but the burden is a unique and inner assurance that he must serve Jesus Christ with all of his life.

The call to full-time Christian service has no alternative. God does not say to a young person I will call you to serve me full-time if you cannot get a better job. The call to full-time Christian service carries the weight of "ought" or "must." When a young person is called into full-time Christian service, he must obey. There is no alternative.

2. *The call to full-time Christian service involves desire.* A man knows he is called of God when his greatest desire is to serve Jesus Christ with every part of his life. This involves his will; it is surrendered and he wants to spend all of his time serving Jesus Christ. Usually the call to full-time Christian service comes to those who are actively involved in the bus ministry, teaching Sunday School or perhaps being a deacon in the local church. They have enjoyed their experience so much that they want to serve God with all of their heart and all of their time.

Jeremiah experienced the burning desire to preach the Word of God. Someone told him he could not preach. He responded, "But His word was in mine heart as a burning fire shut up in my bones, and I was weary with forebearing, and I could not stay (keep quiet)" (Jer. 20:9).

For many years I have dealt with young men who are studying for full-time Christian service. The ones that delight me the most are those young men who just have to preach when they enter their freshman year. They are willing to preach in children's church, in the rescue mission or in the nursing homes. When a man has the fire burning in his heart, he will **sometimes go out into the woods and preach to an empty hillside. This is** more than practice; it is preparation for a lifetime of delivering the Word of God.

3. *The call of God is evidenced by fruit.* When God has put his hand upon a young man and separated him to full-time Christian service, there will be corresponding fruit. Therefore, before a council ordains a young man into the full-time ministry, there should be some evidence that God has used his preaching and teaching of the Word of God. Jesus noted, "Ye

have not chosen me, but I have chosen you and ordained you that ye should go and bring forth fruit, and that your fruit should remain" (John 15:16). The word *ordain* means to lay hands upon, and Jesus was indicating that he had chosen people to put His hands upon them to bring forth fruit.

The symbolic laying on of hands at an ordination service indicates that God has put His spirit and influence on the ministry of a young man. When he has preached people have gotten saved. When he has taught the Word of God, people have been followers of Jesus Christ.

CHARACTERISTICS OF THE CALL

Some people are called immediately when they are converted. They know when they pray for conversion, God also wants them to be a minister of the Gospel. Recently in ministerial classes at Liberty Baptist Schools, I asked for a show of hands on this subject. In the classes, only about 10 percent of the students lifted a hand to indicate that they were called into full-time Christian service at the same time they were saved. That suggests that most young people were called into full-time Christian service at some later time in their Christian life.

Some people receive a sudden and clear call to the ministry. They have been serving Jesus Christ, but in one experience (such as a youth camp) or in one sermon, God impressed upon them to be a full-time Christian servant. Their call to full-time Christian service became an event that was life-changing. They surrendered for full-time Christian service, and from that moment on, they were no longer the same.

On the other hand, the call of God has come gradually to many other servants as the light of a new day gradually lights up the sky. They begin to feel a burden for the ministry as they serve the Lord. Each time they preached or taught, their desire grew to teach or preach again. Their call to full-time Christian ministry was a gradual call.

Again I ask the students at Liberty how they were called into full-time Christian service. Approximately 10 percent say they were called suddenly, while 90 percent indicate the call came gradually.

VIEWS OF THE CALL TO FULL-TIME MINISTRY

W. T. Purkiser in speaking for the position of the Church of the Nazarene states concerning a "call": "it is a definite call; it is a personal call; it is a call to service which can be rendered according to the ability of the called; it is a real challenge; and to refuse it is to go against God's will."[1]

T. Harwood Pattison suggests that a "call" to the service of God is always a call from Him, that a young man who has this "call" has entered the first step in the Christian ministry. "The true man enters the ministry not for the sake of what he can get out of it, but for the sake of what it can get out of him." Pattison then lists how the "call" comes and how it can be recognized.

---

[1]Purkiser, W. T., ed., *Exploring Our Christian Faith,* Beacon Hill Press: Kansas City, MO., 1960, pp. 455, 456.

UNDERSTANDING THE CALL TO FULL-TIME SERVICE

1. How it comes:

(1) Suddenly and unexpected with some unquestionable sign.

(2) Gradually like the dawn of a new day. "Without any question the "call" to preach comes to many a young man with his conversion.

2. How it can be recognized.

(1) When it is plainly the work of the Holy Spirit. "Separate me Barnabas and Saul for the work whereunto I have called them."

(2) Plain by the providential leading of God. "Because a man has failed elsewhere is no reason why he should conclude that he will succeed in the ministry."

(3) Rigid self-examination. Challenge the purity of the motives.

(4) Must be influenced by the judgment of Christian friends and the will of the church to which he belongs.

(5) Ability to preach and the willingness of people to listen.[2]

A. H. Strong concludes that, "the candidate ("Called") himself is to be first persuaded (I Cor. 9:16)—"For though I preach the gospel, I have nothing to glory of; for necessity is laid upon me; yea, woe is unto me, if I preach not the gospel (I Tim. 1:12)—"And I thank Christ Jesus, our Lord, who hath enabled me, in that He counted me faithful, putting me into the ministry." But, secondly, the church must be persuaded also, before he can have authority to minister among them (I Tim. 3:2-7; Titus 1:6-9).[3]

W. B. Riley, pastor of First Baptist Church, Minneapolis, noted fundamentalist during the first half of this century, gives three tests:

1. Compulsion should take the form of conviction.

2. Competence is a prominent evidence. II Tim. 2:24 "apt to teach."

3. Church's observation of fit characteristics.[4]

Perhaps the most complete help in counseling on our subject can be given by William S. Plumer. Though this book was written in 1874 it has some keen insights into our solutions. He states:

1. All are not called. All are bound to glorify God and serve their generation.

2. God alone can call anyone.

3. The greater part of mankind are not called. No wicked man is called.

4. The scriptures do in many ways require that every minister in God's house shall be called to his office by the Lord. Num. 18:7; Deut. 18:20; Isa. 6:8; 11:2, 3; Ezek. 13:3; Matt. 4:18-20; Acts 13:2; Rom. 1:1; I Cor. 1:1; Tit. 1:6; Heb. 5:4.

5. The judgment of the fathers of the Church in past ages fully

[2]Pattison, T. Harwood, For the Work of the Ministry, American Baptist Publication Society: Philadelphia, PA., 1914, pp. 45-52.
[3]Strong, Augustus H., Systematic Theology, (Three Volumes in one) The Judson Press: Valley Forge, PA., p. 919.
[4]Riley, W. B. Pastoral Problems, Fleming H. Revell Co.: New York, NY., 1936, pp. 12-15.
[5]Plumer, William S., Pastoral Theology, Harper & Brothers: New York, NY., 1874, pp. 24-35.

coincides with these teachings of scripture. Vinet says, "We must be called of God . . . whether external or internal; the call ought to be divine."

    6. It is a great and undeserved honor to be put into the sacred office.

    7. Yet, great as the honor is, it does not puff up a good man.

    8. Some bad men have entered the ministry.

    9. What is the call.

If a "call" is real it will gain strength by time and test.[5]

Even though there is confusion in some circles about the call of God to full-time Christian service, there is little doubt in the mind of one who has been called. It is an inner assurance that God's hand is upon his life for a special purpose. The confusion usually comes from those who are not called. Perhaps a few questions would be helpful to guide those who are struggling with the call of God.

    1. Has the person been genuinely converted?

    2. Is the person growing in his Christian life?

    3. Are his motives pure?

    4. Does he possess the physical and mental ability to serve Jesus Christ? (If a candidate has disabilities that would hinder his service, we can seriously question if God has called him into full-time Christian service. However, God has called people with disadvantages, therefore it is their duty to demonstrate and prove the call of God.)

    5. Does the candidate have a love for people and the church of Jesus Christ?

    6. How has the candidate evidenced his burden to preach and teach the Word of God?

    7. How have people in his church and Christian friends responded to his call? (When people around the candidate do not feel he has been called to Christian service, he should demonstrate that he has been called of God.)

    8. What success or fruit has the candidate had in Christian service? (Everyone has to begin somewhere and perhaps the candidate has not had any outward success. This does not mean he has not been called, but he should demonstrate within a reasonable length of time his call of God by the fruit in his ministry.)

    9. What preparation does the candidate have for full-time Christian service and is he willing to attend Bible institute, Christian college, or a seminary to get the best possible preparation for life? (A candidate does not have to have training from a Christian college, but he must have a desire to be the best trained servant possible. When it is evident that a candidate is by passing further training for some reason such as laziness, fear or another known reason, we should counsel him regarding his problem. Those who are called should have the best training possible and not be satisfied with their present service, while at the same time closing future doors because of lack of training.)

CONCLUSION

The call of God into full-time ministry is not the call to salvation, although it includes that. The call into full-time ministry is not the Great Commission to go into all the world, although it includes that. The call of God into full-time ministry is not the knowledge that all men are lost and need salvation, although it includes that.

The call of God into full-time ministry is exactly that. It is God calling a young man to win souls, build churches, teach the Bible and serve Jesus Christ. A man knows he is called because of the burden God gives him to reach the lost. He knows God has given him a desire to preach. He has the inner assurance that he is to serve God. Just as he knows the fire is hot and up is up, so he knows God has called him to preach the gospel and build a church. He responds as did Isaiah, "Here am I, send me."

CHAPTER ELEVEN

UNDERSTANDING HOW TO DISCOVER AND DEVELOP SPIRITUAL GIFTS

Those who serve Jesus Christ do so through the spiritual gifts that have been given to them. If a person is going to be an effective leader, he should understand the Bible teaching on gifts and should have a fairly clear understanding of what gifts he has and how to use them.

But many have known little or nothing about spiritual gifts, yet have been effective servants of Christ. It's not that they violated the Scriptural teachings on gifts. It's not that they were unable to articulate the principle on spiritual gifts in biblical phraseology. They knew the wisdom and power of God. They learned how to serve God effectively, and they were fruitful in their service. They used the principle of spiritual gifts without being able to articulate them.

Many have been used by Christ who were not aware of gifts. That does not place a premium on ignorance. Those who study carefully the principles of spiritual gifts will be saved from making some serious experiential mistakes. They will serve Christ more knowledgeably; hence they will make fewer mistakes in their lives and in the lives of others. They have the potential of being more fruitful for Christ.

THE DEFINITION OF SPIRITUAL GIFTS

Before we can understand what a spiritual gift is, we must first understand what it is not. A spiritual gift is not merely the aid of the Holy Spirit, although the Holy Spirit is an aid to every Christian. A spiritual gift is not a place in the ministry, although God will guide us to a place where we use our gifts. Spiritual gifts are not the same thing as the fruit of the Holy Spirit, nor are the spiritual gifts the same as Christian character or Christian service. Though sometimes related, a spiritual gift is not simply a natural ability through which God works. Spiritual gifts are not tied with any particular age group, i.e., children's worker or youth pastor. A spiritual gift is not what man does for God but rather what God accomplishes through man.

Spiritual gifts are discussed primarily in three passages of Scripture, Romans 12:3-8; I Corinthians 12-14; Ephesians 4:7-11. These Scriptures suggest gifts dealing with a spiritual ability or capacity. Spiritual gifts are given to men (I Cor. 12:11) and these men are in turn given to the church (Rom. 4:11). It is important to remember that "every man hath his proper gift of God" (I Cor. 7:7).

Lewis Sperry Chafer wrote "The gift which is wrought by the Spirit is an expression of the Spirit's own ability rather than the mere use of human qualities in the one through whom he works."[1] These gifts are given not according to our spirituality but according to the will of the Holy Spirit.

CONTROVERSY AND SPIRITUAL GIFTS

One of the areas of great investigation in Christian circles today is the subject of spiritual gifts. The recent growth of pentecostal denominations and widespread influence of the neopentecostal movement has popularized a view of gifts differing from the position of most fundamentalists. Many evangelicals have begun to propose unusual suggestions in their writings on church renewal. The end result is a state of confusion for the young Christian who wants to develop and use their spiritual gifts in the service of Christ. This situation demands a closer look at the Scriptures.

As we list the gifts identified in the above passages, we come to understand there are two kinds of gifts, *sign gifts* and *serving gifts*. The miraculous sign gifts were present in the first century to confirm apostolic revelation but are no longer to be expected today. This concept is understood as we consider the scaffolding principle. When you build a building, it is necessary to erect a scaffolding to aid construction. When the building is built, the scaffolding is removed. The sign gifts were the spiritual scaffolding that God used as His authority to build the church. When the authority of the written Word of God was complete, God took the scaffolding down. There are several reasons why God has removed the sign gifts from Christian experience today.

First, these gifts were first given as a sign to the Jews. As the church was made up primarily of Jews, signs were necessary to demonstrate that the Temple worship and sacrifice were no longer required. As we entered an age of ministry primarily geared at Gentiles, signs became less important, "For the Jews require a sign and the Greeks seek after wisdom" (I Cor. 1:22). Today, the church is founded on Christ the wisdom of God as presented in the Word of God. Second, during the first century, the apostles were primarily communicating an oral tradition (II Thess. 2:15). As a result, sign gifts gave confidence to the church to discern what was the Word of God and what was a message from a false apostle (Heb. 2:3, 4, II Cor. 12:11, 12, Rev. 2:2). A third consideration concerning signs gifts is a recognition that the prophets and apostles were the foundation of the church (Eph. 2:20). These men were the channel of signs and miracles. When they passed off the scene, so did their signs. After the church was founded and the Scriptures were written, they were no longer needed. By the end of the first century, it was impossible for men to be living who qualified to be apostles (Acts 1:21-22). Paul taught tongues would cease (I Cor. 13:8), with the completion of the cannon of Scripture (i.e., "that which

[1]Lewis Sperry Chafer, *Systematic Theology Volume VI: Pneumotology* (Dallas, Texas: Dallas Seminary Press, 1974, p. 216.

is perfect"—I Cor. 13:10).

Today God is still giving his serving gifts to his disciples. These are part of the tools he has provided to help us accomplish the task of world evangelization. Also they are given for our ministry with other Christians that we might help build up the body of Christ.

THE GIFTS OF THE HOLY SPIRIT

SIGN GIFTS	SERVING GIFTS
(no longer available)	Pastor—Eph. 4:11 Teacher—Eph. 4:11 Evangelist (Church Planters) —Eph. 4:11
Apostle—Eph. 4:11	Helps—I Cor. 12:28
Prophet—Eph. 4:11	Ministry—Rom. 12:7 Administration (Business)— I Cor. 12:18
Healing—I Cor. 12:9	Ruling (Church Leadership) —Rom. 12:8
Tongues—I Cor. 12:10	Wisdom—I Cor. 12:8
Miracles—I Cor. 12:10	Knowledge—I Cor. 12:8
Interpretation of Tongues—I Cor. 12:10	Faith—I Cor. 12:9 Prophecy—Rom. 12:6 Giving—Rom. 12:8
Discerning of Spirits— I Cor. 12:10	Exhortation—Rom. 12:8 Showing Mercy—Rom. 12:8 Love—Rom. 12:9

THE DEVELOPMENT OF GIFTS

1. *The Principle of Embryonic gifts.* The Bible teaches that when Jesus ascended to the Father, he gave spiritual gifts to all (Eph. 4:8). When we receive Christ as our personal Savior, that is the moment we receive our spiritual gifts (I Cor. 12:13) because the Holy Spirit who placed us into Christ also gave us the ability to serve Him. Actually, these gifts are latent or embryonic and must be developed. Usually these gifts do not come to light until later in our Christian life.

BECOMING A LEADER

2. *The Principle of Seeking the best gifts.* We are commanded to "Desire earnestly the best gifts", (I Cor. 12:31) which implies we can seek those gifts that have not come to light yet in our life. If we desire a gift, it is probably an evidence that we have the gifts in latent form.

3. *The Principle of Preparation.* Gifts differ both in nature and quality, but none of us possess a perfected gift. Not everyone has the same measure of the same gift. That means a gift can grow in its usefulness. A new Sunday School teacher can grow in effectiveness. Also, a person can get more gifts than what he thinks he now possesses. (See point #2) Spirituality may come in an instant, but maturity takes time. Maturity is learned. Therefore, a Christian needs to take the initiative to prepare himself for service for God. With his initiative, his spiritual gifts are growing. The apostle Paul lived eleven years from his conversion on the road to Damascus until his first missionary journey from Antioch. During that time of preparation, he did not dry up spiritually without a public ministry. God's call to service is God's call to prepare to serve.

4. *The Principle of the Hot Poker.* The development of our gift is usually related to the gifts of others. The poker becomes hot as it gets close to the coals of the fire, so our gift is perfected as we serve closely with others who have the same gift. Several Scriptures suggest gifts are developed in relation to the ministry of another gifted individual (I Tim. 4:4; II Tim. 1:6; Rom. 1:11). A teacher becomes a better teacher by listening to good teaching. A preacher will become a better preacher by sitting under good preaching. The same is true for singers, soul winners and any other thing we might attempt to serve God with.

5. *The Philip Principle.* The Philip Principle recognizes the potential for spiritual growth even to the point of discovering additional gifts (bringing them to light) after conversion. This may also be the development of latent spiritual gifts. Obedience in a smaller spiritual gift leads to a greater use of the gift. This is seen in the ministry of Philip. As a faithful layman, he was selected to fill the office of a deacon in the early church (Acts 6:5). Later he began to preach as the early church was scattered in the persecution (Acts 8:5). By the end of the Book of Acts, Philip had established a reputation as an evangelist. (Acts 21:8).

THE DISCOVERY OF SPIRITUAL GIFTS

The desire of every Christian should be the discovery and development of their gifts (I Cor. 12:31). Each of us has at least one gift (I Pet. 4:10). Some have suggested that every Christian may have as many as three or four gifts. It is our responsibility to discover those gifts and to use them.

This is first accomplished by *knowing yourself.* Know your likes and dislikes. What sort of things come easier or harder for you? It is a good practice to take spiritual inventory from time to time.

Secondly, you must *be willing to do anything.* By God's will there are certain limitations on what you can or cannot do. Do not let additional self-imposed limitations prevent you from having a great ministry. That thing you are unwilling to do may be the one thing big enough to prevent God from using you.

Thirdly, *be active.* Don't hold off doing anything until you find your gift. It is much easier to steer a moving vehicle than a parked car. God can guide and direct your life and ministry better as you are actively serving Him.

A great man once said, "You should do everything possible until forty, then settle down and do one thing well for the rest of your life".

Step four involves an element of risk. *Attempt to use what you think God has given you.* If you are wrong, it will become evident to you, but if you are right, starting to use that gift will bring a sense of satisfaction knowing you have taken the first step of ministry.

In the fifth place, *we develop our spiritual gifts by self determination.* Naturally it will take some time before our gift is polished and perfected, but in the interum it can be used to accomplish the will of God. Every Christian should seek to improve the effectiveness of their gift and thus improve the effectiveness of their ministry. We can improve our effectiveness by taking courses, reading books, learning from others, plus many other ways of training. This does not prevent ministry before the gift is perfected, for using an undeveloped gift is one of the ways we will polish it.

Sixth, seek the counsel and advice of other mature Christians. They will prevent you from going down dead end streets. "Where no counsel is, the people fall, but in the multitude of counselors there is safety" (Prov. 11:14). Even in the case of the apostle Paul, God used other prophets and teachers, the mature Christian leaders in the church at Antioch, to direct him on his first missionary journey (Acts 13:1-2). Presumably, this was how Paul learned he possessed the gift of evangelist (church planter). Your pastor, Sunday School teacher or spiritual friends may be able to see God's working in your life when you cannot.

In the seventh place, *we discover and develop our gift by analyzing our desires.* If God has given a gift, it is probably accompanied by an inner desire to exercise it. The man who has a gift of teaching probably wants to teach and gets a great deal of satisfaction out of teaching. Most Christians have a pagan concept of God, that He is one most desirous of making life miserable by forcing us to do the one thing we could never enjoy. In contrast David wrote, "Delight thyself also in the Lord; and he shall give thee the desires of thine heart" (Ps. 37:4). If you are yielded, what you want to do for God may be evidence of your spiritual gifts and His will for your life.

CHAPTER TWELVE

UNDERSTANDING YOUR SPIRITUAL GIFTS

There are three ideas of gifts in Scripture; (1) a gift of salvation (Rom. 5:15, 16; 6:23); (2) the *enabling gifts* to Christians, (faith, knowledge, wisdom, discernment) (Rom. 1:11; I Cor. 7:7); (3) The specific endowment to special persons, called *task gifts*; (Rom. 12:3-8, I Cor. 12:1-31, Eph. 4:7-11).

The task (serving) gifts; (1) prophecy, Rom. 12:6, (2) teaching, Rom. 12:7, (3) exhortation, Rom. 12:8, (4) shepherding, Eph. 4:11, (5) showing mercy, Rom. 12:8, (6) ministering, Rom. 12:7, (7) helps, I Cor. 12:28, (8) giving, Rom. 12:8, (9) ruling, Rom. 12:8, (10) governments, I Cor. 12:28, (11) evangelist, Eph. 4:11, (12) and hospitality, I Pet. 4:9. Other people add (13) celibacy, (14) martyrdom, and love (I Cor. 13:2).

Some evangelists tend to criticize the Bible teacher because of concern with Bible insight; the evangelist wants results. The teacher tends to call the evangelist shallow or emotional; yet he is needed to preserve the fruits of soul-winning. The mercy showers tend to identify with hurting people that the prophet overlooks as he attacks sin and proclaims righteousness.

When God gave His teaching on spiritual gifts, He did not emphasize them as a methodology for service. God said that we should know our spiritual gifts so we would have harmony in the church. That means that they are given to unify the body of Christ. The three main passages that relate to spiritual gifts are found in Romans 12:3-8, I Corinthians 12:14, and Eph. 4:7-16. These three passages emphasize the unity of the body. The **Roman's passage notes, "So we, being many, are one body in Christ, and every one members of another". (Rom. 12:5). The Corinthian's section** illustrates, "For as the body is one, and hath many members, and all the members of that one body being many, are one body; so also is Christ." (I Cor. 12:12). Then again, "For the body is not one member, but many" (I Cor. 12:14). The Ephesian passage on gifts is introduced, "keep the unity of the spirit in the bond of peace" (Eph. 4:3). Paul reminds the Ephesians that "there is one body" (Eph. 4:4). Finally, verses 12-16 deal with the unity of the church, "the whole body fitly joined together and compacted by that which every joint supplieth . . . maketh increase unto the body by the edifying of itself in love" (Eph. 4:16). From these passages we conclude that everyone should know his gift and the nature of gifts so he will get along with everyone else in the local church. There will be people who for the wrong reasons will be jealous of your gift, ignore your gift or wrongly judge your motives. Every church needs a correct understanding of the different gifts of each member so that everyone will respect one another and work with one another in love.

BECOMING A LEADER

The following list of seven gifts are listed in Rom. 12:6-8. Even though there are more gifts than these, this list is suggestive of those that should be operative in every church. Paul mentions prophecy and ministering first and second because these gifts are reflective of the office of pastors and deacons; the two offices of a local church. However, the following list is changed in order because most pastors are also teachers.

SEVEN GIFTS TO PRODUCE UNITY

1. *Prophecy:* (Rom. 12:6, I Cor. 12:10, 28, 14:3, Eph. 3:11). The person who has this gift has "the ability to proclaim God's truth." The ability to predict the future (I Sam. 9:9) and to be a channel of revelation (Eph. 2:20) foreteller is not operative today. Paul explains, "He that prophesieth speaketh unto men to edification, and exhortation and comfort (I Cor. 14:3). *Strengths:* sensitive to the reputation of God, (2) first to see and denounce sin, (3) understands the sinful motive of man and lack of toleration for hypocrisy, (4) direct and frank, (5) wants outward evidence of conviction, (6) tests results of person before listening to Him. *Weaknesses:* (1) accused of not caring for individuals, (2) judged harsh, (3) uncomfortable in discussion-teaching, (4) difficulty adjusting to softer spirits, (5) crowd oriented. *Dangers:* (1) dependent on sermon for ministry, (2) overlooks individual needs, (3) pride.

2. *Teaching.* The person with this gift has "the ability to accurately make clear God's truth so all can understand it." (Rom. 12:7, I Cor. 12:28, Eph. 4:11). Many laymen have this gift, but when applied to pastors, not God's qualification, "Some". (Eph. 4:11). *Strengths:* (1) desire to study and classify truth, (2) feels his gift is foundational, (3) presents truth systematically, (4) concerned about learning, (5) concerned with accuracy of Scripture and has little toleration for misinterpretation, (6) listens to those who have correct knowledge, (7) sensitive to Bible illustrations. *Weaknesses:* (1) More interested in interpretation than application, (2) lacks practical faith. *Dangers:* (1) proud of knowledge, (2) concentration on details, rather than life, (3) more concerned for truth than individuals.

3. *Exhortation.* (Rom. 12:8) The person who has this gift has "the ability to stimulate faith in others and motivate others to a practical Christian life." *Strengths:* (1) encouraged when he sees results in others, (2) excited about practical principles, (3) interprets his experience into principles, then validates them with Scriptures, (4) comfortable ministering to one person or a group. (5) grieved over sermons that are not practical. *Weaknesses:* (1) gives direction to those who are not willing to receive it. (2) accused of taking Scripture out of context, (3) reluctant to win souls if can't follow-up. *Dangers:* (1) discouraged with lack of progress in listeners, (2) ministers for his selfish purposes, (5) people tell them symptoms and not real problems.

4. *Gift of Giving.* (Rom. 12:8, I Cor. 13:3) The person who has this gift has "the ability to invest material resources in other persons and ministers to

further the purpose of God." *Strengths:* (1) the ability to organize his personal life to make money, (2) desires to give quietly and secretly, ('Don't tell") (3) enjoys giving out of sense of need, rather than being begged, (4) sincere desire to see ministry grow, (5) sensitive to quality, (6) involved with giving i.e. prayer, work, etc. (7) becomes a role-model.

Weaknesses: (1) others feel he gives for an outward impression, (2) others feel he over-emphasizes money, (3) perceived as being selfish. *Dangers:* (1) pride, (2) measures other's spirituality by their prosperity, (3) insensitive to needs of others because of their lack of personal discipline.

5. *Gift of Serving/Ministering/Helps.* (Rom. 12:7, I Cor. 12:28) The person with this gift has "the ability to serve God by ministering to the physical and spiritual needs of others." Usually, those in the office of deacon (diakona) have the gift of serving (diakonia). *Strengths:* (1) enjoys manual projects or practical service, (2) serves without fanfare, but needs appreciation, (3) senses physical and financial needs of others, (4) works for immediate goals (not necessarily long-range projects), (5) gets satisfaction out of completing projects. *Weaknesses:* seems to be more practical oriented, (2) insensitive to the lack of involvement by prophets or teachers in practical projects, (3) others wrongly interpret their good works. *Dangers:* (1) pride, (2) critical of non-practical church leaders, (3) bitter if not recognized, (4) critical of steps of faith that appear unpractical.

6. *Gift of Ruling/Government/Administration/Organization.* (Rom. 12:8, I Cor. 12:28) The person with this gift has "the ability to perceive needs, organize and administer programs, then evaluate the results in light of biblical objectives". *Strengths:* (1) the ability to see the overall picture and think of long-range objectives, (2) the ability to delegate tasks to other people, (3) task oriented, rather than person or need oriented, (4) the ability to counsel and motivate others regarding the task, (5) tends not to be a perfectionist, but rather judges task by objectives. *Weaknesses:* (1) appears to want to get out of work because he delegates, (2) appears insensitive to people and inflexible in God's work because he is committed to long-range goals, (3) may be perceived as a glorified bureaucrat. *Dangers:* (1) power-hungry, (2) uses people to accomplish his goals (manipulation), (3) will use anyone (in spite of character flaws or doctrinal errors) to get job done.

7. *Gift of Showing Mercy.* (Rom. 12:8) The person with this gift has "the ability to locate those in distress and express sympathy to give spiritual help." *Strengths:* (1) the ability to empathize with those who have problems that affect their spirituality so that they desire the healing that is available, (2) place greater emphasis on emotional or spiritual needs than on physical need, (3) has rapport or identity with individuals or group. *Weaknesses:* (1) perceived as offering help when it is not wanted, (2) perceived as being too intimate with people to whom he is ministering, (3) attracts to himself those with emotional problems, the retarded, the handicapped, and social misfits. *Dangers:* (1) lacks firmness in dealing with people, (2) life may be emotionally based, (3) resents others who are not sensitive to inner needs.

BECOMING A LEADER
SEVEN PRINCIPLES LEADING TO UNITY

Be aware of the following principles regarding spiritual gifts that can help lead to unity in the local body. Each of these principles is tied to the correct orientation of spiritual gifts.

Gift Gravitation. Just as the positive pole on a battery attracts the positive pulse in electricity, so the Bible teaches that "like attracts like."This is seen embryonically in the law of creation where, "each produced after its kind" (Genesis 1:12, 21). Those with the gift of teaching, usually find their greatest fulfillment in studying under those who have the gift of teaching. As an illustration, Dallas Seminary is a unique type of seminary that seems to attract young men with an embryonic gift of teaching. They gravitate toward that seminary where their gift is enhanced, and they graduate to minister their gift of teaching. This is also called "gift colonization" by Larry Gilbert, whereby those with similar gifts tend to colonize together. As we view churches, certain independent fundamental churches tend to attract people with a gift of prophecy. The preacher who is always denouncing sin and upholding righteousness attracts the over-bearing father who tends to denounce that which is wrong in the family and holding up the rules of the family.

Gift Assimilation. This principle means that people tend to assimilate the gift of those who minister to them, "like produces like". Those with the gift of teaching tend to produce that gift in others. The biblical basis for gift assimilation is, "Wherefore I put thee in remembrance that thou stir up the gift of God, which is in thee by putting on of my hands" (II Tim. 1:6). The Apostle Paul also teaches this truth in I Tim. 4:14, "Neglect not the gift that is in thee, which was given thee by prophecy, with the laying on of the hands of the presbytery." As a young man sits in an Independent Baptist church and hears his pastor exercise his gift of prophecy (a strong emphasis on condemnation and upholding of righteousness), the young man learns to preach by that role model. He becomes a "prophet" with a strong ministry of denouncing sin and upholding righteousness. In the same way, the pastor with an evident gift of evangelism tends to attract Sunday School teachers and bus workers who have the same gift of soul-winning.

Gift Intrusion. Those who are guilty of this principle try to make every one fit into his mold or to use his gift. He is guilty of gift intrusion, for he tries to get people to use a gift that is not theirs. The pastor who preaches soul-winning so strongly that everyone tries to be the same type of soul-winner as him, may be guilty of gift intrusion. Also the pastor with an evident gift of mercy showing that is exercised in counseling, may expect all of his Sunday School teachers to be mercy-showers. Larry Gilbert calls this "gift imposing", which carries the negative idea of imposing on other people that which is not their indigenous gift.

Gift Manipulation. When one person tries to use a spiritual gift that is not indigenously his, he is guilty of gift manipulation. One occasion the author held an evangelistic crusade in Granite City, Illinois where he preached a five night revival crusade. He tried to exercise the gift of prophecy/evangelism, but to his knowledge no one was saved through that crusade. That took place in 1958 when he first began his teaching ministry at Midwest Bible College, and he learned experientially that he did not have the gift of prophecy/evangelism. Even though on occasions many people have been converted under his ministry, it was when he exercised his teaching gift, rather than when he tried to fill the role of prophet/evangelist. When he tries to exercise abilities that he does not have, it is *gift manipulation.*

Twenty-five years later (1983), the author added an evangelistic crusade to his calendar. The more he prayed about the meeting, the more uncomfortable he became with the prospect of *gift manipulation.* Finally he was convinced that he should not go preach the crusade. He called the pastor and explained his inner conviction, that he was not an evangelist. Therefore both men agreed that the meeting should be cancelled.

Gift Ignorance. Some people are apparently ignorant of their gift and seem to function perfectly well without knowing the technical identification of their spiritual gift. However, the Bible exhorts them to find their gift, "Now concerning spiritual gifts, I would not have you to be ignorant" (I Cor. 12:1) A person may be an effective servant without cognitively knowing his spiritual gift or how to use it. These people have become effective through experimentation or modeled a gift that they saw in another person. This is not the most effective way to find one's gift, but many have found their gift this way. The problem with experimentation and/or modeling is that: (1) one may waste time while he is finding his gift, (2) it leads to mistakes, hence a person could permanently harm his Christian service, and (3) a person might not become as ultimately effective as he might have become if he ministered in confidence. Mistake (trial and error) do not usually teach you how to live a positive life; they teach you negative principles to avoid in life.

Gift Imitation. Some who have thought they have found their gift through trial and error or by role modeling of someone they have admired, may have wrongly tried to minister a gift that they did not have. While that person may produce some spiritual fruit, they may be attempting to serve in a capacity where they do not have the ability to serve God. They are simply imitating a spiritual gift rather than exercising it.

Gift Confidence. Christians who know their spiritual gifts and how to use them are usually the most effective servants of Jesus Christ. They usually make the fewest mistakes, have more confidence in their service for Christ, and have a better attitude about their service. These people do not serve Christ out of guilt, nor are they workaholics. They serve Christ knowing that they are using the spiritual gifts that He has given them in a way that they should be used.

BECOMING A LEADER

CONCLUSION

You should know your gifts so you will be a confident servant of Christ. When you minister from assurance, you will not be jealous of others, nor will you be anxious of your own service. Then in the second place, when everyone else knows the biblical teaching on spiritual gifts and they have identified their gift, they also can work harmoniously with the whole body. *God has blessed a unified church with his presence (Matt. 18:20) and with his power (Acts 2:1-4).

LINCOLN CHRISTIAN COLLEGE AND SEMINARY